1 BETTER ENGLISH EVERY DAY

Language for Living

PAUL J. HAMEL

Los Angeles Unified School District
Santa Monica College

HOLT, RINEHART and WINSTON, INC.

Fort Worth • Chicago • San Francisco
Philadelphia • Montreal • Toronto
London • Sydney • Tokyo

LIBRARY OF CONGRESS CATALOGING IN PUBLICATION DATA

Main entry under title:

BETTER ENGLISH EVERY DAY 1 Language for Living
Includes appendices

1. English Language Textbook for foreigners   I. Hamel, Paul
PN6120.2.S89   1984   808.83'1   83–082148

ISBN 0-03-069601-1

Printed in the United States of America
6 7 8 9 0 1 2 3 4 5   066 18 17 16 15 14 13 12 11 10

To two very special people,
Rene and Rita Landry

ACKNOWLEDGMENTS

Grateful acknowledgments are due to the many people who have encouraged me in writing this series. In particular I am indebted to Nancy Loncke for her invaluable contributions to this series in its early stages.

Special thanks to Elaine Kirn for her sound advice, for helping develop the format and for doing detailed editing. I would especially like to thank Tim Welch, Laura Welch, and Anne Boynton–Trigg for coordinating the production of the series; Pat Campbell, Nancy Cook, Linda Mrowicki, and Jean Zukowski/Faust for editing; Larry Layton for the book design; Frank Ridgeway and Betty Darwin for the art; Shelah Harris and Online Graphics for the typesetting; and Becky Evans and Penny Yost for layout.

Special thanks also goes to the administrators, teachers, and students of Fairfax Community Adult School, Santa Monica City College, Jewish Vocational Service, and the Refugee Employment Training Project for their comments, suggestions, and assistance in developing the lessons.

I am especially grateful to David Chaille for his valuable ideas, insights, and for introducing me to publishing.

Last but not least, I am very grateful to George Gati for his editing, patience, understanding, and putting up with me during the many long hours it took to complete this series.

CONTENTS

INTRODUCTION
TO THE TEACHER

Better English Every Day is a three-book series designed for adult students of English as a second language. It presents the grammar, vocabulary, and language competencies necessary for getting along in an English-speaking country. While students are learning survival skills, they practice the four skills—listening, speaking, reading, and writing. The major aim of the series is to teach English for everyday living, enabling students to enter the job market and to function successfully at work as well as in the community.

The books are divided into chapters with common themes—a class, shopping, a party, and the like. Within each chapter, "modules" carefully integrate grammatical structures with practical vocabulary in useful situations. After opening with a typical conversation, each module presents student-centered oral activities (pair or group practice) and varied written exercises, in as natural a context as possible.

Because the series is directed at low-level students with practical rather than academic goals and interests, it aims at simplicity. Essential grammar principles are quickly presented at the level of the student. The series emphasizes language use. It recycles grammatical structures again and again, with review and new vocabulary in changing contexts.

The books carefully balance survival and vocational situations. Most of the vocabulary presented in work situations is also applicable in other contexts, and vice versa.

Special features of *Better English Every Day* include a section for writing practice (printing and cursive letters) at the beginning of Book 1, a phonic or spelling lesson at the end of each chapter, self-checking pair activities in which students respond to one another while looking at different sections of the same page, and "Challenge" activities which provide students with the opportunity to go beyond the text.

Although most activities are self-explanatory, teaching notes give suggestions for class presentations and additional activities.

TEACHING NOTES

These teaching notes detail some effective ways of teaching language skills. The basic techniques in these notes offer guidelines and suggestions to help the teacher present lessons in an effective and interesting way. We hope these suggestions will inspire other, more creative techniques.

Listening Comprehension

The teacher may want to use the following techniques to develop effective listening comprehension skills.

1. After introducing key vocabulary words at the beginning of a reading lesson or dialog, slowly read the text aloud to your students before having them open their books. Then ask general comprehension questions. At the end of the reading lesson, dialog, or follow-up review exercise, read the text again at normal speed. The students should not be allowed to read along; they should concentrate on listening.
2. Give frequent short dictations. (See section on dictation.)
3. When doing drills or question-and-answer exercises, have students cue one another whenever possible. This forces them to listen to each other and become accustomed to different accents.
4. Have students work in pairs and groups so that they can listen and respond to one another on a more personal level. (See section on pairing and grouping.)
5. When practicing dialogs or role-playing, occasionally have pairs of students stand back-to-back so that they must understand each other without the aid of non-verbal cues.
6. Invite a guest speaker, the principal, the school nurse, a police officer, etc., to be interviewed in class so that the students can hear other accents and intonations. Before allowing the students to interview the speaker, prime the class by discussing the kinds of questions they will ask. By practicing the questions beforehand, students will be less embarrassed about asking questions or making mistakes.
7. Give students the opportunity to listen to different examples of spoken English through music, games, movies, slide presentations, etc.

Dictation

Do not underestimate the usefulness of dictation. It can be a very effective tool for practicing the four language skills. It is especially useful as a warm-up exercise at the beginning of the class period to review previously covered materials. Frequent short dictations focusing on commonly used words and expressions used in simple sentences, and stressing function words, such as articles, prepositions, pronouns, and auxiliary verbs, will do much to improve students' writing and spelling. Once students become accustomed to the simple dictations presented in this series, you may want to vary the dictation format to keep interest high. As an example, try the following:

1. Dictate six questions.
2. After the students have written six questions in their notebooks, ask six volunteers to write the questions on the chalkboard.
3. Have six other students read and correct the questions.
4. Have six more volunteers go up to the chalkboard and write the answers to the questions.
5. Have students read and correct the answers.
6. Discuss additional possible answers to the questions.

Other Suggestions:

1. Dictate the answers, and then have students write the questions.
2. Dictate single words that students must use in complete sentences.
3. Dictate jumbled sentences that students must put into correct word order.

Preliterate Component

A supplementary chapter at the front of Book 1, IN THE BEGINNING, is designed to give students the opportunity to practice forming the letters of the alphabet. You may want to stress the material in class, use it as a review, or have students simply practice on their own at home. You will have the best results by not moving too quickly through this chapter. Do no more than one or two pages a day.

Pronunciation and Spelling

Although teaching pronunciation and spelling should play a very important role in the beginning English class, it has too often been ignored. Despite many irregularly spelled words, some basic pronunciation and spelling rules can be taught early on to improve reading and writing skills. Keep such lessons short, introduce them frequently, and review them repeatedly. Here are some suggestions on how to begin teaching pronunciation in Chapter 1:

1. When you begin teaching simple consonants (b, d, f, g, h, j, k, l, m, n, p, r, s, t, v, w, x, y, and z), teach the sounds of the letters rather than their names. Although the names of the letters are important in spelling, they should come later once the basic sounds have been learned and associated with their written forms.
2. Make or buy alphabet cards.
3. Hold the cards up and say the sounds of the letter. Then name an object that begins with the sound. It is very helpful to show a picture of the object with the written word below it.
4. Have the students repeat the sounds and words.
5. Have students think of words beginning with the

sounds, i.e., "b" for "boy," "d" for "dog," "f" for "food," etc. This is an excellent way to judge how much English a new group of students knows.
6. Introduce only one short vowel, "e."
7. Make or buy a second set of consonant cards.
8. So that students can begin to build words, place each set of consonants on either side of the vowel "e," creating a three-letter word. A chalkboard tray is a convenient place do this.
9. Have students read the word.
10. Replace or switch around the consonants to make new words. Do not be overconcerned about creating meaningless words. Remember, this is practice for combining *sounds* into words.
11. On the next day, teach the short vowels by associating their sounds with objects or gestures as in the following example:
a = the "baa" sound of a lamb;
e = the vowel in "10" (show ten fingers);
i = a gesture of rejecting or refusing something disgusting;
o = rubbing your stomach and saying "aaah" to indicate that you have just eaten something delicious;
u = a boxer hitting somebody in the stomach.
12. Introduce the five short vowels into the word grid described in item 8 above.
13. Practice making new words.
14. On subsequent days, introduce "c," "sh," "ch," and "th" in the same manner.
15. Over a longer period of time, gradually build new words with consonant blends ("sp," "sk," "nd," etc.), long vowels ("ai," "ee," "ea," "oa," "ie," "ue," etc.), the silent final "e," and other groups that appear in the pronunciation lessons of the book.

Other Suggestions:

1. Use visuals, objects, pictures, and gestures as much as possible for constant reinforcement.
2. Do not overburden the students with too much pronunciation or spelling material at once. Do not teach more than one pronunciation lesson per day.
3. Irregularly spelled words should be taught separately from words that follow rules. A good way to teach them is through frequent dictation.

Vocabulary

The following suggestions are only a few of those to be kept in mind when teaching vocabulary.

1. Use as many flash cards, objects (realia), and pictures as possible in order to reinforce the words visually. This will help hold interest and aid students in remembering new vocabulary.
2. Define the words and give many contextual examples in sentences, expressions, and situations. Also help define and contrast the new vocabulary with synonyms, antonyms, and homonyms.

3. When selecting vocabulary, concentrate on practical, high-frequency, functional vocabulary and expressions.
4. Do not overburden your students with too many vocabulary items at any one time. Introduce ten or so new words per lesson.

Suggested Activities:

1. Flash Cards: Write new words on 5'' x 8'' index cards and use them in your lessons. Daily add a few new words. Mix them up and use them for review. Continually add to them until you have developed a word bank. Use the cards for pronunciation practice, drills, recognition, dictation, spelling bees, and other word games.
2. Conversation Practice: Cut out pictures describing everyday life from newspapers and magazines and paste them on construction paper. Then, on the back of each picture, write four or five vocabulary words represented in the picture (a noun, a verb, an adjective, and a preposition). Even if many more words could be added, limit the number.

   Divide the class into pairs or small groups and distribute the pictures. (See the section on pairing and grouping.) Tell the students to use the vocabulary on the back of the pictures to identify the objects and discuss what is happening. As a variation, write a list of question words on the chalkboard and have students use them in asking each other questions. Walk around the classroom, listening and correcting errors and spending time with the weaker students. Let groups exchange pictures to continue the exercise.
3. Tic–tac–toe: Draw a tic–tac–toe grid and fill it in with vocabulary. Divide the class into two teams, each team being assigned the symbol "X" or "O." Then flip a coin to determine which team begins. Have the students take turns in an orderly fashion by going down the rows. Tell the first student of the first team to use any word from the grid in a sentence. If the sentence is correct, replace the word with the team's symbol, X or O. Otherwise, leave the word. Go on to the first person on the other team. Continue in this manner until one team wins by having three consecutive X's or O's in a row vertically, horizontally, or diagonally. Keep score by giving one point for each game won. After each game, replace all the words in the grid with a different category of words, such as all prepositions, all verbs, all antonym pairs, etc.
4. Crossword Puzzle: Draw a grid and words on the chalkboard. Divide the class into two teams and flip a coin to determine which team goes first. Have the first student of the first team go to the chalkboard and write a word that uses one letter of an existing word in the crossword. If the word fits and is correctly spelled, give one point for every letter of the new word. If the word is incorrect, erase it and go to the opposite team.

Pair Practice

Pairing exercises give the students time, especially in large classes, to practice important speaking skills. Organizing students to work together can be somewhat frustrating at the start, but once they clearly understand what you expect of them, subsequent pairing activities usually proceed smoothly. Most pair practice exercises consist of simple substitution or transformation drills that you can also use for drilling the class as a whole.

1. Explain that this kind of exercise is to allow students to practice their *speaking* skills, not their writing skills. Tell students to put away all writing materials.
2. Have each student choose a partner. You will probably have to go around the classroom and pair students the first few times you do this activity. Encourage students to pair up with different partners each time.
3. Indicate the material you want the students to practice.
4. Walk around the classroom, listening to individual students and correcting any errors you hear. This provides an excellent opportunity to spend time with your weaker students.

Reading

Some Suggestions:

1. Before reading the dialog or passage, introduce the new vocabulary and grammatical structures. For effective visual reinforcement, use the chalkboard, flash cards, and pictures. Give many contextual examples of new words.
2. Read the text. The students should not see the text at this point. Use this time as a listening comprehension exercise. (See section on listening comprehension.)
3. Ask simple comprehension questions using question words such as "what," "where," "when," and "why."
4. Read the text a second time, with the students reading along. As you read, tell the students to underline any unfamiliar vocabulary and expressions.
5. Discuss the vocabulary and expressions the students have underlined.
6. Ask more detailed comprehension questions.

Other Suggestions:

1. Have students read the text silently. Then ask basic comprehension questions.
2. Have students retell the story in their own words.
3. After asking detailed comprehension questions, have students ask their own detailed questions of each other.
4. On another day, give a short dictation based on part of the text. (See section on dictation.)
5. Prepare a handout of the text with some of the

vocabulary items missing (cloze–type exercise). Have students supply the missing words.

6. Have students write a story modeled on the text or dialog.
7. If possible, have students change the story from dialog to text or vice versa.
8. Do a read–and–look–up exercise. Have students read a sentence silently, then try to repeat as much of the sentence as they can without looking at the book.
9. Prepare a handout of a text or dialog with some of the words missing. Read the text aloud and have students fill in the missing words as they read along.

Dialogs

Some Suggestions:

1. Before presenting the dialog to the class, select and introduce any vocabulary items and structures that the students are not familiar with.
2. Read the dialog once for general comprehension. You may want to let the students read along.
3. Have students close their books.
4. Read the first line aloud, and then have the students repeat it. If necessary, have them repeat it several times for correct pronunciation and intonation.
5. Teach the second line (rejoinder) in the same manner. If the line is too long, present it in segments.
6. Repeat the first line, having a student respond with the rejoinder. Then reverse roles.
7. Select two students to repeat the two lines.
8. Teach the next two lines in the same manner.
9. Return to the beginning of the dialog and review it to the point where you left off.
10. Continue to the end of the dialog. (If the dialog is very long, select only one part. Do not try to teach dialogs which are more than 8 lines.)

Other Suggestions:

1. Write the first part of the rejoinder on the chalkboard and have students come up to write the second part.
2. Give part of the dialog as a dictation on a subsequent day.
3. As a written quiz, prepare a handout of the dialog with some of the key vocabulary items missing. Have students fill in the blanks from memory.
4. Have students write their own dialog modeled on the text.
5. Have students rewrite the dialog as a narrative.
6. Adapt the dialog to be used as the basis of a role–playing exercise. (See section on role–playing.)

Writing

Expose students through short frequent exercises to writing that is closely related to the vocabulary, structures, and topics you have already taught. Exercises should also be varied, practical, and related to students' daily lives.

Be careful not to overwhelm students. Begin this program with simple exercises such as addressing envelopes and writing postcards, notes, and shopping lists. Such initial practice will give students time to learn the most commonly used words which are also the most irregularly spelled, such as pronouns, articles, prepositions, and auxiliary verbs. Once students have learned the basics, gradually build up to longer and more complex exercises.

Suggestions:

1. Assign writing exercises that reinforce or review previously learned material.
2. When giving a writing assignment as homework, reserve the last part of the class period for writing. This will allow you to walk around the classroom to make sure everyone understands the assignment.
3. When correcting the students' papers, correct only serious mistakes in structure and spelling. Praise the correct use of recently taught vocabulary and structures.
4. If you find mistakes that several students are making, note them and teach a special lesson based on these mistakes.
5. Include the entire class in the correcting process by copying the incorrect sentences taken from their papers onto the chalkboard or a handout. Have a class discussion on how best to correct the mistakes.
6. Have students rewrite their corrected exercises in their notebooks.
7. Keep a list of spelling errors to be used in a future dictation.

Grammar

Some Suggestions:

1. Present grammar in order of increasing difficulty.
2. In introducing grammar, use situations, visuals, and graphics to give students several different ways of understanding the structure.
3. Present and reinforce grammar in the context of survival skills, situations, activities, stories, and games. For example, when teaching the possessive *of,* also teach the names of food containers (carton *of* milk, can *of* soup, etc.).
4. End all lessons, or do follow–up reviews, with communicative activities, such as role–playing, incorporating the grammatical structure. For example, after teaching *some* and *any*, role–play ordering food in a restaurant. For teaching prepositions, set up an obstacle course in the classroom and have students direct each other through it. (See the section on role–playing.)
5. When presenting drills, vary them constantly

whenever possible. Cue responses with gestures, objects, pictures, and flash cards.

6. In non-academic courses, minimize the use of grammatical terms. For instance, most students are interested in learning how to *use* the structures rather than in knowing the difference between transitive and intransitive verbs.

7. Constantly review previously taught grammar. Reintroduce it in another context, contrast it with another grammatical structure, or build it into another lesson.

Role-Playing

Use role-playing to expand your lessons and reinforce vocabulary and structures. Before expecting students to perform successfully in role-playing exercises, consider the following:

1. Discuss the situation beforehand so that students can familiarize themselves with the topic as well as with necessary vocabulary and structure.

2. Teach a dialog as a primer, or allow students to prepare themselves in pairs or small groups. (See section on pair practice.)

3. Have students do each role-playing exercise twice, the first time with teacher participation and the second time without.

4. Encourage students to vary situations and be creative.

5. Don't over-correct. Note major mistakes; discuss and correct them later. To practice active listening, have the class note errors, too.

6. Discuss the role-playing exercise afterward for students' reaction and interpretations.

Some Basic Situations:

Asking and giving street directions; looking at and asking questions about a new apartment; calling the telephone operator for information; buying an item in a store; going on a job interview; speaking to a doctor, dentist, or pharmacist; getting a driver's license; introducing and meeting people at a party; making or canceling an appointment; leaving a message; asking a postal clerk about correct postage; cashing a check; opening a checking or savings account at a bank; ordering food at a restaurant; etc.

General Suggestions

1. Create an atmosphere where students are not afraid to make mistakes. Simple communication is more important than speaking perfectly.

2. Encourage students to use what they have learned in class in their speech. Encourage them to speak to one another in English during their breaks and free time. You might even reserve a special "English table" or area in your classroom where students can practice while having a snack or a cup of coffee.

3. Be eclectic. Use any method, technique, or combination of methods that work for you and your students.

4. Use as much variety in your lessons as possible.

5. Space out your best lessons and activities throughout the course to keep interest high. Don't empty your entire "bag of tricks" early on.

6. Make and collect as many teaching aids (visuals, objects, handouts) as possible. Store them for future use.

7. Require your students to bring dictionaries to school and use them often.

IN THE
BEGINNING...

PRINTING AND WRITING PRACTICE
- Printing Small and Capital Letters
- Cursive Writing

READ

Aa Bb Cc Dd Ee Ff

Gg Hh Ii Jj Kk Ll

Mm Nn Oo Pp Qq Rr

Ss Tt Uu Vv Ww Xx

Yy Zz

READ

Aa Mm Hh Qq Yy Tt Ll Gg Dd

Oo Uu Pp Jj Cc Ff Bb Ee Ii

Kk Nn Rr Vv Ss Ww Zz Xx

COPY   *Print the small letters.*

a a a

g g g

q q q

b b b

d d d

p p p

n n n

m m m

h h h

COPY *Print the small letters.*

u u u

v v v

w w w

y y y

i i i

j j j

f f f

t t t

r r r

COPY *Print the small letters.*

c c c

o o o

x x x

z z z

s s s

e e e

k k k

a b c d e f g h i j k l

m n o p q r s t u v

w x y z

COPY *Print the capital letters.*

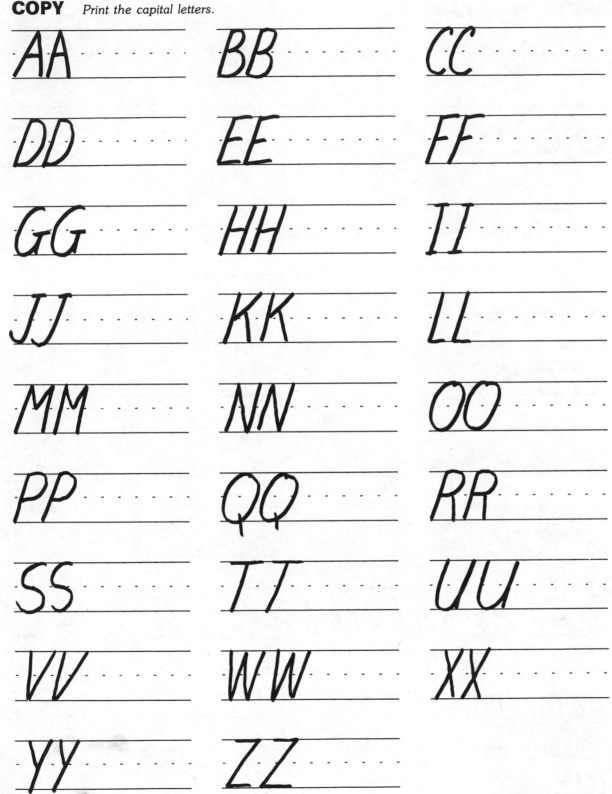

AA BB CC

DD EE FF

GG HH II

JJ KK LL

MM NN OO

PP QQ RR

SS TT UU

VV WW XX

YY ZZ

WRITE *Copy the words.*

picture

clock

chalkboard

map

chair

window

pen

door

pencil

book

desk

table

notebook

paper

WRITE *Match the small and the capital letters.*

1. B   p   2. N   u   3. S   z   4. R   j

   D   q   M   n   L   s   I   l

   P   g   H   m   Z   l   L   f

   Q   b   U   v   X   k   J   i

   G   d   V   h   K   y   F   r

5. A   u   6. T   f   7. A   a   8. H   v

   E   c   F   t   C   e   N   m

   C   o   I   j   O   b   W   w

   O   e   J   i   E   c   Y   h

   U   a   Y   y   B   o   M   n

WRITE *Write the small letters next to the capital letters.*

A a   E   I   M   Q   U   Y

B   F   J   N   R   V   Z

C   G   K   O   S   W

D   H   L   P   T   X

WRITE *Write the capital letters next to the small letters.*

A a   e   i   m   q   u   y

b   f   j   n   r   v   z

c   g   k   o   s   w

d   h   l   p   t   x

WRITE   *Write the small letter or the capital letter.*

| A | a | E | _____ | I | _____ | M | _____ | Q | _____ | U | _____ | Y | _____ |

| B | b | _____ | f | _____ | j | _____ | n | _____ | r | _____ | v | _____ | z |

| C | _____ | G | _____ | K | _____ | O | _____ | S | _____ | W | _____ |

| _____ | d | _____ | h | _____ | l | _____ | p | _____ | t | _____ | x |

READ   *Notice the difference:* **a** = a,   **g** = g.

small letters: a b c d e f g h i j k l m
                     n o p q r s t u v w x y z

capital letters: A B C D E F G H I J K L M
                       N O P Q R S T U V W X Y Z

WRITE   *Match the letters.*

1. h	*w*	2. b	*d*
n	*h*	d	*q*
w	*v*	q	*b*
v	*m*	p	*g*
m	*n*	g	*p*

3. A	*u*	4. t	*F*
E	*a*	f	*y*
C	*e*	i	*J*
O	*c*	j	*I*
U	*o*	y	*T*

READ

Aa Bb Cc Dd Ee Ff

Gg Hh Ii Jj Kk Ll

Mm Nn Oo Pp Qq Rr

Ss Tt Uu Vv Ww Xx

Yy Zz

READ

Xx Zz Ww Ss Vv Rr Nn Kk

Ee Bb Ff Cc Jj Pp Uu Oo Dd

Gg Ll Tt Yy Qq Hh Mm Aa Ii

COPY   *Write basic cursive strokes.*

eeeee

llllll

llllll

Oeeeee

mmmm

uuuuuuu

ccccc

ffffff

nnnn

sssss

COPY *Write the cursive small letters.*

a aaaaaaa

d dddddd

g ggggggg

f fffffff

n nnnn

m mmm

x xxxx

v vvvv

e eeeeeee

l lllllll

COPY *Write the cursive small letters.*

i iiiiiii

j jjjjjjjj

b bbbbbb

f ffffffff

h hhhhh

k kkkkkk

t tttttt

u uuuuuu

y yyyyyy

COPY   *Write the cursive small letters.*

w wwww

s sssssss

p ppppp

z zzzz

r rrrrrr

c cccccc

o oooooo

READ

These letters begin and end on the line:

a c d e f g h i j k l m n o p q r s t u x y z

These letters begin on the line, but **don't** *end on the line:*

b   o   v   w

WRITE   *Copy these words. Be careful with* *b*, *o*, *v*, *and* *w*.

1. *table*

2. *chalkboard*

3. *book*

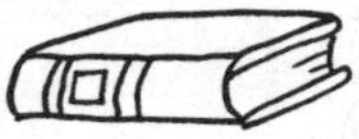

4. *tool box*

5. *door*

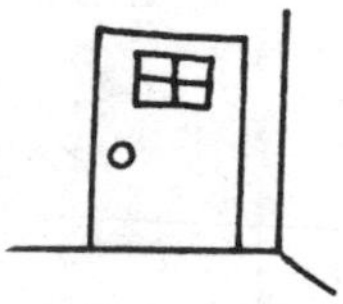

6. *broom*

7. *window*

8. *workbench*

WRITE   *Copy the alphabet in cursive writing.*

a b c d e f g h i j k l m n o p q r s t u v w x y z

WRITE   *Copy the alphabet backwards in cursive writing.*

z y x w v u t s r q p o n m l k j i h g f e d c b a

WRITE   *Copy the words in cursive writing.*

COPY   *Write the cursive capital letters.*

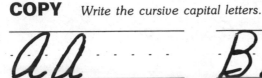 

Cc

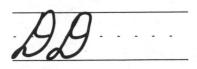 Ee

 Hh Ii

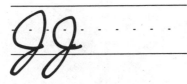 Kk Ll

 Nn Oo

 22

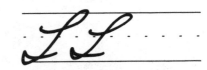

  Uu

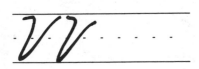 Ww Xx

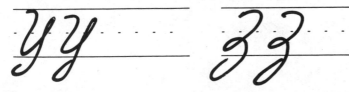 33

WRITE   *Match the small and the capital cursive letters.*

1. K   x
   X   k
   Z   l
   L   s
   S   z

2. R   j
   I   l
   L   f
   G   i
   F   r

3. B   p
   D   q
   P   g
   Q   b
   G   d

4. V   h
   U   n
   H   m
   M   u
   N   v

5. A   u
   E   r
   C   o
   O   e
   U   a

6. Y   j
   G   i
   I   f
   F   t
   J   y

7. A   e
   C   a
   O   w
   E   o
   W   c

8. H   v
   N   m
   W   w
   V   h
   M   n

WRITE   *Write the small cursive letters next to the capital letters.*

A a   E ___   I ___   M ___   Q ___   U ___   Y ___

B ___   F ___   G ___   N ___   R ___   V ___   Z ___

C ___   H ___   K ___   O ___   S ___   W ___

D ___   H ___   L ___   P ___   J ___   X ___

WRITE   *Write the capital cursive letters next to the small letters.*

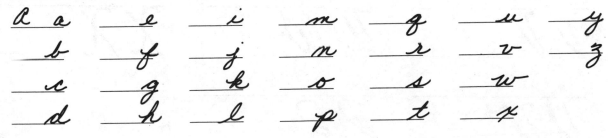

A a   e ___   i ___   m ___   q ___   u ___   y ___

b ___   f ___   j ___   n ___   r ___   v ___   z ___

c ___   g ___   k ___   o ___   s ___   w ___

d ___   h ___   l ___   p ___   t ___   x ___

WRITE *Write the small or the capital letter.*

a _____ *E* _____ *I* _____ *m* _____ *2* _____ *U* _____ *Y* _____
_____ *b* _____ *f* _____ *j* _____ *n* _____ *r* _____ *v* _____ *z*
e _____ *G* _____ *K* _____ *O* _____ *S* _____ *W* _____
_____ *d* _____ *h* _____ *l* _____ *p* _____ *t* _____ *x*

WRITE *Write the small and capital cursive letters.*

A_____	_____e	I_____	_____m	Q_____	_____u	Y_____
B_____	_____f	J_____	_____n	R_____	_____v	Z_____
_____c	G_____	_____k	O_____	_____s	W_____	_____a
_____d	H_____	_____l	_____p	_____t	_____x	_____g

WRITE *Write the small letters of the alphabet in cursive.*

_____

_____

_____

WRITE *Write the capital letters in cursive.*

_____

_____

_____

WRITE   *Circle the letter that is different from the others.*

1. a A *a* *(e)* *a*
2. E e *(c)* *E* *l*
3. l L i *L* *l*
4. *o* Q O o *O*
5. *u* *U* u U V
6. B b d *B* *b*
7. *c* c C e *C*
8. D *D* *d* b d
9. f *F* F E *f*
10. G g *g* *G* *g*
11. n H *H* h *h*
12. J i j *j* *J*
13. *k* k K *K* h
14. I *L* L l *l*
15. *m* *M* n M m
16. N n *n* h *n*
17. P q p *p* *P*
18. *Q* q *Q* p Q
19. *r* *R* r v R
20. S s *s* c *S*
21. *t* t f T *J*
22. V v v *V* *x*
23. w W *W* *w* *u*
24. *X* X *x* x k
25. Y y v *y* *Y*
26. *Z* z z *y* *z*
27. Z *z* *y* *z* Z
28. *Y* y *Y* v *y*
29. *x* *x* *n* X *x*
30. *u* *W* W w *w*
31. v *x* *v* V V
32. u *w* *U* U *u*
33. *J* *t* *t* *F* T
34. *L* *s* s *s* S
35. *R* *R* *v* *r* r
36. Q *2* *g* *g* *g*
37. *P* *p* *P* *g* *p*
38. *O* *o* O o *Q*
39. N *n* *N* *m* *m*
40. *M* *m* *n* M *m*
41. *L* *l* *e* l L
42. *K* *k* K *k* *h*
43. *g* J *j* i *j*
44. *i* i I J *J*
45. *h* k *H* *h* h
46. *G* G *g* *g* *g*
47. *f* F *l* *F* *f*
48. *E* *e* *l* *E* e
49. *D* b *d* *d* D
50. *c* C c *e* *C*
51. *d* b *l* *B* *B*
52. *A* *d* *A* *a* a

WRITE   *Copy the names of the people in cursive.*

Here are some people in this book.

1. *ROY BARNS*   2. *NANCY BARNS*   3. *BOBBY BARNS*   4. *MARIO CORRAL*

_____

5. *MARIA CORRAL*   6. *MONA BOULOS*   7. *YEN CHU*   8. *STEPHEN BRATKO*

9. *SAMI HAMATI*   10. *MIKO TAKAHASHI*   11. *DAVID FERNANDEZ*   12. *PAUL GREEN*

_____

13. *RITA LANDRY*   14. *RAYMOND MONTE*   15. *ROBERTO MONTE*   16. *JOANNE YATES*

_____

17. *JAMES FULLER*   18. *TAN TRAN*   19. *LAN TRAN*   20. *ANN PORTER*

_____

Welcome to the ESL Class

COMPETENCIES	•	**Meeting and Introducing People**
GRAMMAR	•	***to be (am, is, are)***
	•	***this/that; these/those***
	•	**Indefinite Article**
	•	**Singular and Plural Nouns**
VOCABULARY	•	**Classroom Items**
	•	**Numbers (1–12)**
PHONICS	•	**Consonants**

LISTEN

It's break time at an adult school. Sami Hamati and David Fernandez are at the catering truck.

David: Oops! Excuse me.
Sami: That's OK.
Caterer: Coffee?
Sami: Uh-huh. How much is it?
Caterer: It's sixty cents.
Sami: Here you are.
Caterer: What are those?
David: They're potato chips.
          How much are they?
Caterer: They're fifty cents.
David: Here you are.
Caterer: And here's your change.
David: Thanks.

UNDERSTAND   *Circle True or False.*

1. Coffee is 60 cents at the catering truck.   (True)   False
2. It's break time at the adult school.   True   False
3. Potato chips are 35 cents.   True   False
4. The caterer is a student at the adult school.   True   False
5. "Uh–huh" means "yes."   True   False

PAIR PRACTICE   *Talk with another student about the pictures below.*

Student 1: What's that?
Student 2: It's ....
Student 1: How much is it?
Student 2: It's .... cents.
Student 1: Here you are.
Student 2: Thanks.

coffee
60 cents

lemon soda
50 cents

milk
70 cents

juice
40 cents

Student 1: What are those?
Student 2: They're ....
Student 1: How much are they?
Student 2: They're ....
Student 1: Here you are.
Student 2: Thanks.

cookies
45 cents

potato chips
50 cents

sandwiches
2 dollars

apples
20 cents

READ

PAIR PRACTICE

Talk with another student. Practice the variations above.

Student 1: Oops! ....
Student 2: ....

PAIR PRACTICE

Talk with another student. Practice the phrases below.

Student 1: Here's/Here are your ....
Student 2: Thank you.
Student 1: You're welcome.

1. coffee
2. apples
3. juice
4. potato chips
5. milk
6. lemon soda
7. sandwiches
8. cookies
9. change
10. ....

READ

MENU			
Coffee	$ .60	Apples	$ .20
Lemon Soda	.50	Potato Chips	.50
Juice	.40	Sandwiches	2.00
Milk	.70	Cookies	.45

PAIR PRACTICE

Use the menu above.

Student 1: How much is/are ....
Student 2: It's/They're ....

LISTEN

David Fernandez and Sami Hamati meet.

> *David:* Hi! I'm David Fernandez.
> *Sami:* I'm Sami Hamati.
> *David:* I'm pleased to meet you.
> *Sami:* Pleased to meet you, too.
> *David:* I'm in the wood shop class.
> What about you?
> *Sami:* I'm an ESL student.
> *David:* Oh, the bell! The break's over.
> *Sami:* See you later.
> *David:* Yes, see you tomorrow.
> *Sami:* Good-bye!
> *David:* Bye!

UNDERSTAND *Circle True or False.*

1. David Fernandez is in the wood shop class.   True   False
2. Sami Hamati is in the wood shop, too.   True   False
3. David and Sami are students.   True   False
4. David Fernandez is in the ESL class.   True   False
5. David is pleased to meet Sami; Sami is pleased to meet David.   True   False
6. "Good-bye" means "Bye."   True   False

PAIR PRACTICE   *Talk with other students.*

Student 1: Hello, I'm ....
Student 2: Hi! I'm ....
Student 1: Pleased to meet you.
Student 2: Pleased to meet you, too.

READ

PAIR PRACTICE   *Use the variations above with other students.*

Student 1: Hello, I'm ....
Student 2: Hi! I'm ....
Student 1: .... to meet you.
Student 2: .... to meet you, too.

READ

PAIR PRACTICE   *Use the variations above with another student.*

Student 1: Good-bye.
Student 2: ....

LISTEN

Yen Chu's a new student in the ESL class. She meets Roy Barns. He's the teacher. She meets the students, too.

Mr. Barns:	Please come in.
Yen:	I'm a new student.
Mr. Barns:	Welcome to the class.
Yen:	Here's my registration card.
Mr. Barns:	Thank you.
Yen:	You're welcome.
Mr. Barns:	Please sit down.
(to the class)	This is Yen Chu.
	She's a new student.
	She's Chinese.
	She's from Hong Kong.

UNDERSTAND   *Circle True or False.*

1. Roy Barns is a new student.   True   False
2. Yen Chu is a new student.   True   False
3. They are in the ESL class.   True   False
4. "Please come in" means "Please sit down."   True   False
5. "You're welcome" means "Welcome to the class."   True   False

PAIR PRACTICE *Talk with another student. Practice the structure below.*

Student 1: This is ....
            She's/He's ....
Student 2: Welcome to the class.

1. Yen Chu/Chinese
2. David Fernandez/in the wood shop class
3. Sami Hamati/Egyptian
4. Yen Chu/a new student
5. Sami Hamati/in the ESL class
6. Yen Chu/from Hong Kong
7. Mr. Barns/a teacher
8. Mr. Barns/in the classroom
9. Sami Hamati/from Egypt

READ

GROUP PRACTICE *Each student reads one part.*

WRITE   *Fill in the blanks with the correct words from the box below.*

over	Glad	I'm	this	to	
	you	too	Good-bye		

Yen Chu meets Wanda Bratko and Maria Corral, two students in the ESL class.

Yen: Hello. (1) _____I'm_____ Yen Chu.

Wanda: Hi. (2) _____ Wanda Bratko.

And (3) _____ is Maria Corral.

Maria. (4) _____ to meet you, Yen.

Yen: (5)_____ to meet you, (6)_____.

Wanda: Welcome (7)_____ the class.

Yen: Thank (8)_____.

Maria: Oh, the bell!

Wanda: The class is (9)_____.

Yen: Bye.

Maria: (10)_____.

Wanda: See (11)_____ tomorrow.

WRITE   *Match the words to make sentences.*

David Fernandez   is 60 cents.

Juice   's OK.

Sami Hamati   is in a wood shop class.

That   is over.

Coffee   is 40 cents.

The break   is an ESL student.

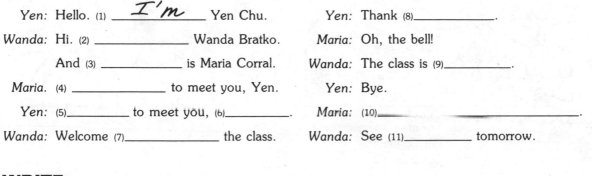

DICTATION   1. *Cover the sentence under each line with a piece of paper.*
2. *Listen and write the dictation on the line.*
3. *Then uncover the sentences and correct your writing.*

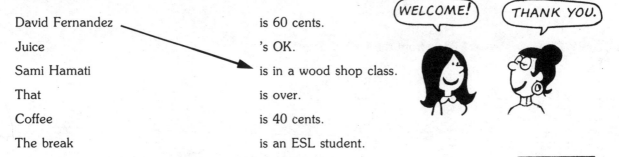

Dear Yen,

1. _____

    I'm Sami Hamati.

2. _____

    I'm a student in the class, too.

3. _____

    Welcome to the ESL class.

4. _____

    See you later in the break.   *Sami*

LISTEN

Sami tells Yen Chu about the ESL class.

Sami: I'm an auto mechanic.
I'm Egyptian.
I'm from Cairo.

He's Roy Barns.
He's the teacher.
He's American.
He's from the United States.

This is Miko Takahashi.
She's a beautician.
She's Japanese.
She's from Tokyo.

These two people are Mario and Maria Corral.
Mario's an electrician and Maria's a cashier.
They're Mexican.
They're from Mexico City.

They're Stephen and Wanda Bratko.
Stephen's an accountant and Wanda's a salesperson.
They're Polish.
They're from Warsaw.

UNDERSTAND   *Circle **True** or **False**.*

1. Roy Barns is an electrician.		True	False
2. Miko is from Tokyo, Japan.		True	False
3. Sami is from Mexico.		True	False
4. Mario is an auto mechanic.		True	False
5. Stephen and Wanda are from Poland.		True	False

PAIR PRACTICE   *Introduce yourself to other students. Walk around the classroom.*

Student 1: Hello, I'm ....
Student 2: I'm ....
Student 1: I'm ....
         I'm from ....
Student 2: Glad to meet you.
Student 1: Glad to meet you, too.

GROUP PRACTICE   *Introduce one student to another. Walk around the classroom.*

Student 1: This is ....
         He's/She's ....
         He's/She's from ....
Student 2: Pleased to meet you.
Student 3: Pleased to meet you, too.

GRAMMAR   The verb *to be*

EXAMPLES

- *Forms of* **be**

I	**am**	Sami Hamati.
He	**is**	a teacher.
They	**are**	in the ESL class.

- *Contractions* (for speech)

I	**'m**	Sami Hamati.
He	**'s**	a teacher.
They	**'re**	in the ESL class.

READ *Make complete sentences with the words in the box below.*

I			the United States.
He	'm		Mexico.
She		from	Canada.
It	's	in	the classroom.
We			a student.
You	're		American.
They			Mexican.

READ

COUNTRIES AND NATIONALITIES

NORTH AMERICA

Canada	Canadian
Mexico	Mexican
United States	American

SOUTH AMERICA

Argentina	Argentinian
Bolivia	Bolivian
Brazil	Brazilian
Chile	Chilean
Colombia	Colombian
Ecuador	Ecuadorian
Guyana	Guyanan
Paraguay	Paraguayan
Peru	Peruvian
Uruguay	Uruguayan
Venezuela	Venezuelan

CENTRAL AMERICA

Costa Rica	Costa Rican
El Salvador	Salvadoran
Guatemala	Guatemalan
Honduras	Honduran
Nicaragua	Nicaraguan
Panama	Panamanian

CARIBBEAN REGION

Cuba	Cuban
Haiti	Haitian
Dominican Republic	Dominican

EUROPE

Austria	Austrian
Belgium	Belgian
Bulgaria	Bulgarian
Czechoslovakia	Czech
Denmark	Danish
Finland	Finnish
France	French
Germany	German
Greece	Greek
Hungary	Hungarian
Ireland	Irish
Italy	Italian
Netherlands	Dutch
Norway	Norwegian
Poland	Polish
Portugal	Portuguese
Romania	Romanian
Russia	Russian
Spain	Spanish
Sweden	Swedish
Switzerland	Swiss
U.S.S.R.	Soviet
Britain	British
Yugoslavia	Yugoslavian

MIDDLE EAST

Iran	Iranian
Iraq	Iraqi
Israel	Israeli
Jordan	Jordanian
Lebanon	Lebanese
Palestine	Palestinian
Saudi Arabia	Saudi
Syria	Syrian
Turkey	Turkish

FAR EAST

China	Chinese
Japan	Japanese
Korea	Korean
Mongolia	Mongolian
Philippines	Filipino

SOUTHEAST ASIA

Cambodia	Cambodian
Indonesia	Indonesian
Laos	Laotian
Thailand	Thai
Vietnam	Vietnamese

SOUTH ASIA

Afghanistan	Afghan
India	Indian
Nepal	Nepalese
Pakistan	Pakistani

OCEANIA

Australia	Australian
New Zealand	New Zealander
Polynesia	Polynesian

AFRICA

Algeria	Algerian
Egypt	Egyptian
Ethiopia	Ethiopian
Ivory Coast	Ivorian
Kenya	Kenyan
Liberia	Liberian
Libya	Libyan
Nigeria	Nigerian
Senegal	Senegalese
Somalia	Somalian
South Africa	South African
Sudan	Sudanese
Tunisia	Tunisian
Uganda	Ugandan
Zaire	Zairian
Zambia	Zambian
Zimbabwe	Zimbabwan

CHALLENGE *Circle the nationalities of the people in your class.*

PAIR PRACTICE   *Talk with another student about the people on the class list.*

Student 1: He/She/.... (name) ....
                         or
            They .... (name) .... and .... (name) ....
            He/She/They ... (occupation) ....
            He/She/They ... (nationality) ....
Student 2: And he/she/they ....

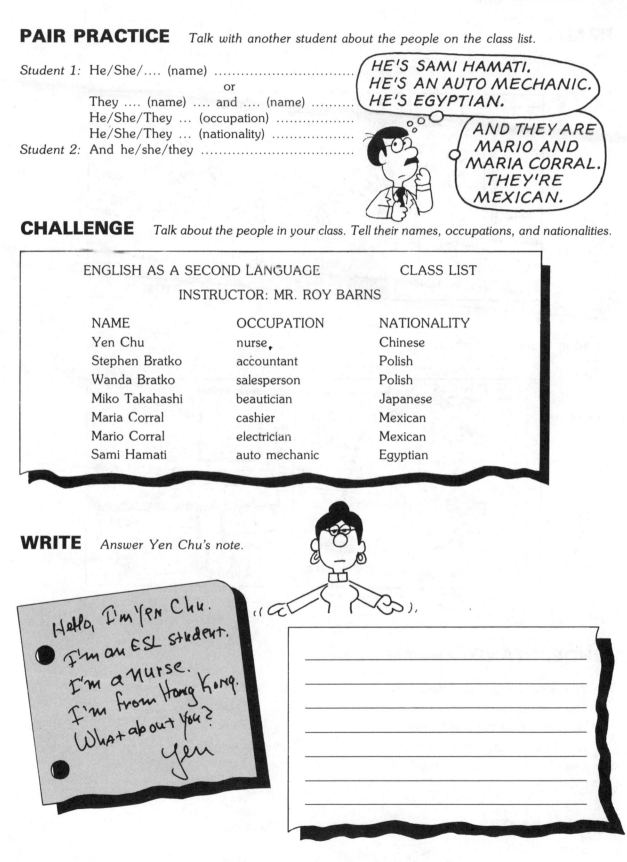

CHALLENGE   *Talk about the people in your class. Tell their names, occupations, and nationalities.*

ENGLISH AS A SECOND LANGUAGE   CLASS LIST
INSTRUCTOR: MR. ROY BARNS

NAME	OCCUPATION	NATIONALITY
Yen Chu	nurse.	Chinese
Stephen Bratko	accountant	Polish
Wanda Bratko	salesperson	Polish
Miko Takahashi	beautician	Japanese
Maria Corral	cashier	Mexican
Mario Corral	electrician	Mexican
Sami Hamati	auto mechanic	Egyptian

WRITE   *Answer Yen Chu's note.*

READ

Sami is in the ESL classroom.

David is in the wood shop.

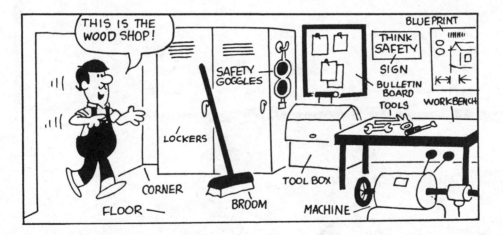

UNDERSTAND   *Circle True or False.*

1. The table is in the ESL classroom.   True   False
2. The tool box is in the ESL classroom.   True   False
3. Mr. Barns is in the wood shop.   True   False
4. David Fernandez is in the wood shop.   True   False
5. Sami Hamati is in the wood shop.   True   False

CHALLENGE   *Find the names of the tools in the picture.*

GRAMMAR   The indefinite article

Singular				Plural			
a	book	**an**	auto mechanic	book	**s**	auto mechanic	**s**
a	tool	**an**	engineer	tool	**s**	engineer	**s**
a	window	**an**	accountant	window	**s**	accountant	**s**

Note: Use **an** before vowel sounds.

WRITE   *Write a or an for the singular and s for the plural. Leave some spaces blank.*

Sami: Hi, David.

David: Oh, hi, Sami.

Sami: Here are Stephen and Mario. They're ____ *X* ____ friend *S* ____.

Mario's _____ electrician and Stephen's _____ accountant _____.

David: Hello.

Mario and Stephen: Hi.

Sami: This is Yen Chu and Maria Corral. They're _____ student

_____, too. Yen's _____ nurse _____ and Maria's

_____ cashier.

David: Pleased to meet you all.

The students: Pleased to meet you, too.

Sami: And here's Mr. Barns. He's _____ ESL teacher _____.

Mr. Barns: Bye! See you all at the break tomorrow.

PAIR PRACTICE   *Talk with another student about the pictures below.*

Student 1: What's this? or What are these?

Student 2: It's / They're ....

1.
2.
3.
4.
5.
6.
7.
8.
9.

WHAT'S THIS?
IT'S A DESK.
WHAT ARE THOSE?
THEY'RE WINDOWS.

LISTEN

0	1	2	3	4
zero	one	two	three	four

5	6	7	8
five	six	seven	eight

9	10	11	12
nine	ten	eleven	twelve

READ

Roy Barns and his son, Bobby, are at home.

DADDY, HELP ME WITH MY HOMEWORK!

WHAT'S FIVE PLUS THREE MINUS ONE?

THAT'S SEVEN.

READ AND WRITE *Do the problems orally.*

$$\begin{array}{cccccc} 1 & 2 & 3 & 4 & 5 & 2 \\ +1 & +2 & +4 & +5 & +2 & +10 \end{array}$$

$$\begin{array}{cccccc} 1 & 2 & 6 & 7 & 12 & 11 \\ -1 & -1 & -3 & -4 & -5 & -2 \end{array}$$

1. Five plus three equals_____.
2. Two minus one equals_____.
3. Four plus two equals_____.
4. Twelve minus nine equals_____.
5. Eight minus six equals_____.

1 + 1 =   6–1 =   5 + 2 =   9–3 =

12–2 =   8 + 3 =   12–11 =   11 + 1 =

10–10 =   10–7 =   5 + 3 =   9–5 =

2 + 2 =   7 + 2 =   11–9 =   4 + 5 =

6. Five plus seven equals_____.
7. One minus one equals_____.
8. Six minus three equals_____.
9. Five plus six equals_____.
10. Seven minus four equals_____.

WRITE   *Fill in the blanks with the words from the box.*

a table	a window	a pen	a chalkboard
a desk	a book	a wall	a picture
a door	a map	the floor	a corner
lights	chalk	a clock	the ceiling

WRITE   *Fill out the survey for your class. Then read it aloud.*

CLASS SURVEY

Instructor: _____ Class: _____ Room: _____

	Number			Number
Asians	_____	Lights		_____
Europeans	_____	Maps		_____
Africans	_____	Doors		_____
South Americans	_____	Desks		_____
North Americans	_____	Tables		_____
Men	_____	Pictures		_____
Women	_____	Clocks		_____
Students	_____	Windows		_____

WORD ORDER   *Write correct sentences with the words below.*

1. *Welcome to this class.*

class.
Welcome
this
to

2. _____

_____

new
I'm
student,
a
ESL
too.

3. _____

name?
your
What's

4. _____

from
I'm
Hong Kong.

5. _____

about
you?
What

6. _____

from?
are
Where
you

7. _____

at
break.
the
you
See

WRITE   *Answer the note above.*

PHONICS   Consonants

LISTEN   *Pay attention to the first sound. Then pronounce the words.*

LISTEN   *In each line, circle the word that begins with the same sound as the first letter of the first word.*

seven	listen	(see)	zero		**pe**n	Brazil	Polish	false
help	what	right	hello		**ro**om	wood	locker	registration
word	Vietnam	write	window		**ta**ble	David	true	chips
juice	yes	Japan	glad		**va**se	bye	one	vocabulary
light	later	room	you		**bo**ok	wall	plus	break
machine	new	me	we		**gl**ad	class	good	work
corner	ceiling	glasses	clock		**se**ven	zero	six	caterer

WRITE   *Listen to the word. Then write the first letter of each word.*

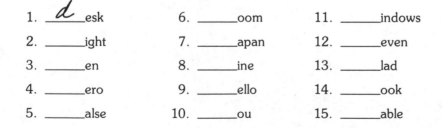

1. *d*_esk   6. ____oom   11. ____indows

2. ____ight   7. ____apan   12. ____even

3. ____en   8. ____ine   13. ____lad

4. ____ero   9. ____ello   14. ____ook

5. ____alse   10. ____ou   15. ____able

Isn't This the Wood Shop Class?

COMPETENCIES	• Greeting and Describing People • Telling Time
GRAMMAR	• *to be* (negative and question forms) • *to be* + adjectives • *where/when* • *in/on*
VOCABULARY	• Common Occupations • Numbers (telephone numbers, years, age) • Emergency Telephone Numbers
PHONICS	• Short Vowels

LISTEN

Joanne Yates speaks to Wanda in the ESL classroom.

Joanne: Is this Room 126?
Wanda: No, it isn't.
Joanne: Isn't this the wood shop class?
Wanda: No, it isn't. This is the ESL class.
Joanne: Where's the wood shop?
Wanda: It's next door.
Joanne: Thank you.
Wanda: You're welcome.

Joanne Yates sees a friend, David Fernandez, in the hall.

Joanne: Hey! David! Wait!
David: Joanne! Hi!
Joanne: How are you?
David: Fine, thanks, and you?
Joanne: OK. Are you a student here?
David: Yeah, what about you?
Joanne: I'm a new student.
David: What class are you in?
Joanne: In the wood shop class.
David: So am I.
Joanne: Great! Where's the wood shop?
David: This way. Come on.

UNDERSTAND   *Circle **True** or **False**.*

1. The wood shop is in Room 126.	True	False
2. The ESL class is in Room 126.	True	False
3. Joanne and David are friends.	True	False
4. David's a new student.	True	False
5. "So am I" means "Me, too."	True	False
6. "Wait!" means "Come on."	True	False

READ

PAIR PRACTICE   Talk with another student. Practice the phrases below.

Student 1: How are you?
Student 2: ...., and you?
Student 1: ...., thank you.

READ

PAIR PRACTICE   Practice the variations above.

Student 1: ....
Student 2: You're welcome.

GRAMMAR   To be in the question and negative forms

EXAMPLES					
Question			**Negative**		
Is	this Room 126?		This	**isn't**	the wood shop.
Are	you a student here?		I	**'m not**	an ESL student.
			We	**aren't**	ESL students.

READ   *Make complete sentences with the words in the boxes below. Make sure they make sense.*

Negative

I	am not	fine.
	'm not	break time.
He		at school.
She	is not	in Room 126.
It	isn't	in the class.
We		the wood shop.
You	are not	in the U.S.A.
They	aren't	here.

Question

Am	I	OK?
	he	break time?
Is	she	in Room 126?
	it	at school?
	we	in the wood shop?
Are	you	in the ESL class?
	they	in the U.S.A?

PAIR PRACTICE   *Talk with another student.*

Student 1: Is this ....?
Student 2: No, it isn't.
Student 1: Where is it?
Student 2: It's ....

IS THIS THE ESL CLASS?

WHERE IS IT?

NO, IT ISN'T.

IT'S NEXT DOOR.

1. ESL class/next door
2. the wood shop class/this way. Come on.
3. ESL class/in Room 127
4. the wood shop class/in Room 126
5. the adult school/next door
6. Room 126/in the room next door
7. Room 127/this way. Come on.
8. ....

PAIR PRACTICE   *Talk with another student.*

Student 1: What class are you in?
Student 2: In ....
Student 1: So am I.

WHAT CLASS ARE YOU IN?

SO AM I.

IN ESL 1.

1. ESL 1
2. the wood shop class
3. ESL 2
4. Room 126
5. Room 127
6. this classroom
7. that classroom
8. ....

WRITE   *Fill in the spaces with the words in the box.*

is	it's	where's
this	isn't	

A student: Excuse me, (1) _____*is*_____ this the ESL classroom?

Joanne: No, it (2) _____.

A student: Isn't (3) _____ the ESL class?

Joanne: No, it (4) _____. (5) _____ the wood shop class.

A student: (6) _____ the ESL class?

Joanne: (7) _____ next door.

LISTEN

Joanne and David are in the hall.

Joanne: Hurry up! We're late for class.
David: No, we aren't.
Joanne: What time is it?
David: It's six thirty.
Joanne: No, it isn't. It's after seven o'clock.
Your watch is slow!

Joanne Yates meets her new teacher, Mr. Fuller.

Mr. Fuller: Hello, David. How are you?
David: Fine, thanks, Mr. Fuller, and you?
Mr. Fuller: Great! And who's this?
David: This is Joanne Yates. She's a new student.
Mr. Fuller: Well, welcome to the class.
Joanne: Thank you. Here's my registration card.
Mr. Fuller: Thanks. Please come in and sit down.

UNDERSTAND   *Circle **True** or **False**.*

1. Joanne is a new student in the ESL class.   True   False
2. Joanne and David are in the wood shop.   True   False
3. Mr. Fuller is a new student.   True   False
4. It's seven o'clock.   True   False
5. Joanne and David are late for class.   True   False

PAIR PRACTICE   *Talk with another student.*

Student 1: Are we .... ?
Student 2: No, we aren't.
            We're ....
Student 1: Oh, yes, you're right.

1. in Room 127/in Room 126
2. late/early
3. in the ESL 1 classroom/in the ESL 2 classroom
4. in the wood shop/next door
5. early/late
6. office/counseling office

WRITE   *Fill in the spaces with* **'m, 'm not, 's, isn't, are,** *or* **aren't**.

It __'s__ OK. I _____ in the ESL class. Yen Chu, Joanne Yates, and David Fernandez

_____ my new friends. Yen Chu _____ in my class, but Joanne and David _____; they

_____ in the wood shop. I _____ in Room 124 and the wood shop _____ next door.

Mr. Fuller _____ the wood shop instructor. He _____ my teacher; Mr. Barns _____ the

ESL teacher. Oh! The time! It _____ 7:15. I _____ late for class. See you later! Bye!

DICTATION   *Cover the sentences under each line. Listen and write the dictation on the line. Then uncover the sentences and correct your writing.*

David,

1. _____
   Hi, David. How are you?

2. _____
   Who's the new student?

3. _____
   Where's she from?

4. _____
   Are you two friends?

5. _____
   See you at the break.

   Miko

WRITE   *Answer Miko's note.*

LISTEN

Wanda Bratko tells Yen Chu about the wood shop.

This is the wood shop.
It's big, clean, and modern.
The machines are noisy, and they're dangerous, too.
The students are careful.

That's Mr. Fuller.
He's the instructor.
He's very helpful.

That's Paul Green.
He's a very friendly man.
He's an apartment house manager
He's retired.
I think he's 48 years old.

They're Raymond and Roberto Monte.
They're twins. They're 24.
Raymond's a truck driver.
I think Roberto's a draftsman.

That's David Fernandez.
He's very smart.
He's a painter.
I think he's 23 years old.

That's Joanne Yates.
She's a new student.
I think she's a telephone operator.

Joanne Yates is single.
So is David Fernandez.
Paul Green is widowed.
Raymond Monte is married, but his brother isn't.

UNDERSTAND   *Circle **True** or **False**.*

1. Paul Green isn't married.	True	False
2. Joanne Yates is retired.	True	False
3. David Fernandez is single.	True	False
4. Paul Green is the instructor.	True	False
5. Raymond and Roberto aren't in the ESL class.	True	False
6. The students are dangerous.	True	False

READ

David speaks to Rita Landry, a student in the wood shop.

Rita: Are you an auto mechanic?
David: No, I'm not.
Rita: Are you a cashier?
David: No, I'm not.
Rita: Are you an electrician?
David: No, I'm not.
Rita: Well, what are you?
David: I'm a painter.

> ARE YOU AN AUTO MECHANIC?
>
> NO, I'M NOT.

PAIR PRACTICE   *Play a guessing game with another student.*

Student 1: Are you a ....?
Student 2: Yes, I am. / No, I'm not.
Student 1: Well, what are you?
Student 2: I'm a ....

> ARE YOU A CASHIER?   NO, I'M NOT.

1. a cashier
2. a nurse
3. a telephone operator
4. an accountant
5. a truck driver
6. an apartment house manager
7. a salesperson
8. a draftsman
9. an ESL student

WRITE   *Answer the questions. Write **Yes, I am.** or **No, I'm not.***

1. Are you single? _____
2. Are you married? _____
3. Are you an instructor? _____
4. Are you widowed? _____
5. Are you retired? _____

6. Are you a student? _____
7. Are you a nurse? _____
8. Are you strong? _____
9. Are you friendly? _____
10. Are you smart? _____

PAIR PRACTICE   *Talk with another student.*

>Student 1: Are you ....?
>Student 2 or 3: Yes, we are. / No, we aren't.
>or
>I am, but he/she isn't.

1. instructors
2. students
3. Vietnamese
4. from Europe
5. single

6. in this class
7. electricians
8. helpful in class
9. late
10. ....

WRITE   *Try to remember the answers from page 49.*

1. Is Paul Green friendly?

2. Is Joanne Yates retired?

3. Are Raymond and Roberto Monte young?

4. Are Paul Green and James Fuller twins?

5. Is Joanne Yates in the ESL class?

6. Are the machines in the wood shop dangerous?

Yes, he is.

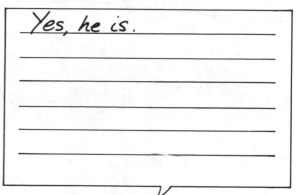

PAIR PRACTICE   *Ask and answer questions about your class.*

Student 1: Is your classroom ....?
Student 2: Yes, it is. / No, it isn't.

1. dirty
2. modern
3. noisy
4. dangerous
5. quiet

6. clean
7. new
8. big
9. small
10. ....

PAIR PRACTICE   *Ask and answer questions about your teacher.*

Student 1: Is the teacher ....?
Student 2: Yes, he/she is. / No, he/she isn't.

1. friendly
2. helpful
3. young
4. married
5. smart

6. careful
7. single
8. strong
9. nice
10. ....

READ

GRAMMAR   *in* and *on*

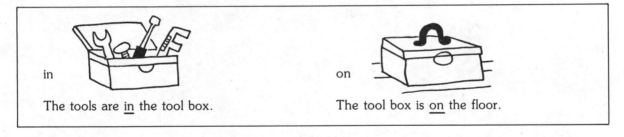

The tools are <u>in</u> the tool box.

The tool box is <u>on</u> the floor.

PAIR PRACTICE   *Talk to another student.*

Student 1: Where's your ....?
Student 2: .... on/in ....

1. pen
2. pencil
3. book
4. notebook
5. desk

6. teacher
7. classroom
8. school
9. home
10. ....

PAIR PRACTICE
Ask and answer questions with another student about the items in the picture below.

Student 1: Where are the ....?
Student 2: They're in/on................
Student 1: Where's the ....?
Student 2: It's in/on.....................

WRITE
Fill in the line with a question or an answer.

Joanne: Where's the tool box?
David: *It's on the floor.*

Joanne: Where are the brooms?
David: They're in the corner.

Joanne: _____?
David: They're on the machine.

Joanne: _____?
David: It's on the book.

PAIR PRACTICE   *Fold this page. Look at only your side.*

Student 1	**Student 2**

Student 1

Listen to the questions. Find the answers in the picture below.

Now you ask the questions.

1. What's on the wall?
2. What's in the desk?
3. Where are the notebooks?
4. Where's the chalkboard?
5. What's on the chalkboard?
6. Where are the pens?
7. Where are the lights?
8. Where's the map?
9. Who's in the room?

Student 2

Ask these questions.

1. What's in the corner?
2. What's on the table?
3. What's in the box?
4. Where's the tool box?
5. Where are the tools?
6. Who's in the picture?
7. What's on the wall?
8. Where's the machine?

Now listen to the questions. Find the answers in the picture below.

FOLD HERE

LISTEN

LOCKER COMBINATION NUMBER

Locker	Right	Left	Right			
1	13	14	15	(thirteen	fourteen	fifteen)
2	16	17	18	(sixteen	seventeen	eighteen)
3	19	20	21	(nineteen	twenty	twenty-one)
4	22	23	24	(twenty-two	twenty-three	twenty-four)
5	25	26	27	(twenty-five	twenty-six	twenty-seven)
6	28	29	30	(twenty-eight	twenty-nine	thirty)
7	40	50	60	(forty	fifty	sixty)
8	70	80	90	(seventy	eighty	ninety)

HERE ARE YOUR NEW COMBINATION LOCK NUMBERS.

READ   *Pronounce the numbers.*

STUDENT	LOCKER	COMBINATION NUMBER		
		Right	Left	Right
David Fernandez	9	35	0	15
Roberto Monte	10	5	18	33
Joanne Yates	11	30	13	24
Paul Green	12	14	8	40
Rita Landry	13	19	90	55
Raymond Monte	14	81	18	69

PAIR PRACTICE   *Ask and answer questions with another student about the combination numbers above.*

Student 1:   What's the combination for locker number one?
Student 2:   It's …. …. ….

WHAT'S THE COMBINATION FOR LOCKER NUMBER NINE?

IT'S THIRTY-FIVE, ZERO, FIFTEEN.

LISTEN   *What's your telephone number?*

5	4	0	-	1	3	4	2
five	four	oh (zero)		one	three	four	two

READ   *Pronounce the telephone numbers below.*

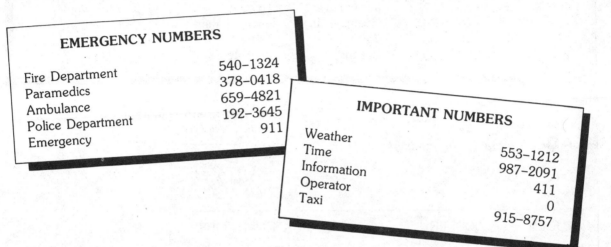

EMERGENCY NUMBERS

Fire Department	540–1324
Paramedics	378–0418
Ambulance	659–4821
Police Department	192–3645
Emergency	911

IMPORTANT NUMBERS

Weather	
Time	553–1212
Information	987–2091
Operator	411
Taxi	0
	915–8757

PAIR PRACTICE   *Talk with another student. Use the numbers above.*

Student 1: What's the telephone number for the/a/an .... ?
Student 2: It's ....

WHAT'S THE TELEPHONE NUMBER FOR THE FIRE DEPARTMENT?

IT'S FIVE-FOUR-ZERO-ONE-THREE-TWO-FOUR.

PAIR PRACTICE   *Ask other students in your class.*

Student 1: What's your telephone number?
Student 2: It's ....

WHAT'S YOUR TELEPHONE NUMBER?

IT'S NINE-FOUR-SIX-FIVE-TWO-ONE-OH.

CHALLENGE   *Find the telephone numbers for these places in your city.*

1. Operator _____ 0 _____
2. Paramedics _____
3. Ambulance _____
4. Police Department _____
5. Fire Department _____
6. Time _____
7. Information _____
8. Weather _____

READ *Tell the time.*

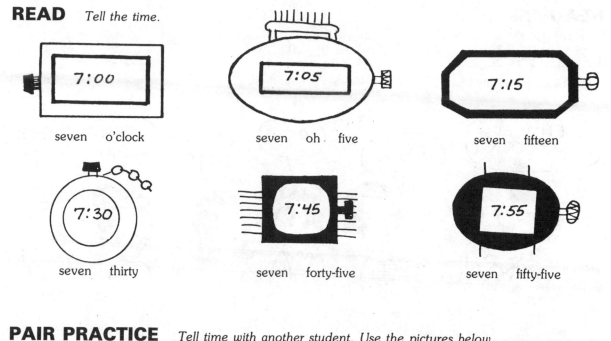

7:00 seven o'clock

7:05 seven oh five

7:15 seven fifteen

7:30 seven thirty

7:45 seven forty-five

7:55 seven fifty-five

PAIR PRACTICE *Tell time with another student. Use the pictures below.*

Student 1: Excuse me, what time is it?
Student 2: It's ....

EXCUSE ME, WHAT TIME IS IT?

IT'S SEVEN THIRTY.

1.

2. 3:15

3. 7:00

4.

5. 8:45

6. 9:50

7.

8. 12:35

9. 2:25

10. 5:10

11.

12.

READ   *Pronounce the years.*

1 9 8 4
nineteen   eighty-four

1 9 0 0
nineteen   hundred

1 9 0 1
nineteen   oh   one

WHEN WERE YOU BORN?

1964.

1952.

1951.

1934.

1948.

Miko   Mario   Maria   Yen   Stephen

WRITE   *Calculate the ages, and then help Mr. Barns fill in his roll book.*

ESL 1 ROLL BOOK

NAMES	AGE
Mario Corral	_____
Maria Corral	_____
Miko Takahashi	_____
Yen Chu	_____
Stephen Bratko	_____

PAIR PRACTICE   *Talk with another student.*

Student 1:   How old are you?
Student 2:   ....
Student 1:   When were you born?
Student 2:   ....

HOW OLD ARE YOU?
WHEN WERE YOU BORN?
TWENTY-THREE.
NINE-TEEN SIXTY-ONE.

CHALLENGE   *Read the ages, and then calculate the year of birth.*

WOOD SHOP ROLL BOOK

Student	Age	Year of Birth
Paul Green	48	_____
Joanne Yates	29	_____
Raymond Monte	24	_____
Roberto Monte	24	_____

READ

WHEN WHERE YOU BORN?

AND YOUR BIRTHDAY?

IN 1964.

ON AUGUST FIFTH.

READ   *Ordinal Numbers*

first	(1st)	sixth	(6th)	eleventh	(11th)	twenty-first	(21st)
second	(2nd)	seventh	(7th)	twelfth	(12th)	twenty-second	(22nd)
third	(3rd)	eighth	(8th)	thirteenth	(13th)	twenty-third	(23rd)
fourth	(4th)	ninth	(9th)	fourteenth	(14th)	thirtieth	(30th)
fifth	(5th)	tenth	(10th)	twentieth	(20th)	one hundredth	(100th)

GRAMMAR   *in / on*

- *We use **in** with months and years, and **on** for dates and days of the week.*

EXAMPLES

I was born	**in**	August.
I was born	**in**	1964.
I was born	**on**	August 5th.
I was born	**on**	August 5, 1964.

- *Here are variations for dates.*

EXAMPLES

| I was born | **on** | the fifth of August. |
| I was born | **on** | Thursday, August 5th. |

READ   *Calendar*

JANUARY	FEBRUARY	MARCH	APRIL	MAY	JUNE
1 2 3 4 5 6 7 8 9 10 11 12 13 14 15 16 17 18 19 20 21 22 23 24 25 26 27 28 29 30 31	1 2 3 4 5 6 7 8 9 10 11 12 13 14 15 16 17 18 19 20 21 22 23 24 25 26 27 28 29	1 2 3 4 5 6 7 8 9 10 11 12 13 14 15 16 17 18 19 20 21 22 23 24 25 26 27 28 29 30 31	1 2 3 4 5 6 7 8 9 10 11 12 13 14 15 16 17 18 19 20 21 22 23 24 25 26 27 28 29 30	1 2 3 4 5 6 7 8 9 10 11 12 13 14 15 16 17 18 19 20 21 22 23 24 25 26 27 28 29 30 31	1 2 3 4 5 6 7 8 9 10 11 12 13 14 15 16 17 18 19 20 21 22 23 24 25 26 27 28 29 30

JULY	AUGUST	SEPTEMBER	OCTOBER	NOVEMBER	· DECEMBER
1 2 3 4 5 6 7 8 9 10 11 12 13 14 15 16 17 18 19 20 21 22 23 24 25 26 27 28 29 30 31	1 2 3 4 5 6 7 8 9 10 11 12 13 14 15 16 17 18 19 20 21 22 23 24 25 26 27 28 29 30 31	1 2 3 4 5 6 7 8 9 10 11 12 13 14 15 16 17 18 19 20 21 22 23 24 25 26 27 28 29 30	1 2 3 4 5 6 7 8 9 10 11 12 13 14 15 16 17 18 19 20 21 22 23 24 25 26 27 28 29 30 31	1 2 3 4 5 6 7 8 9 10 11 12 13 14 15 16 17 18 19 20 21 22 23 24 25 26 27 28 29 30	1 2 3 4 5 6 7 8 9 10 11 12 13 14 15 16 17 18 19 20 21 22 23 24 25 26 27 28 29 30 31

PAIR PRACTICE   *Talk with another student.*

Student 1: When's your birthday?
Student 2: It's ....

CHALLENGE   *Circle the dates of birth of five students in your class on the calendar above.*

READ

AMERICAN HOLIDAYS

DATE	HOLIDAY
January 1	New Year's Day
January 15	Martin Luther King's Birthday
February 12	Abraham Lincoln's Birthday
February 14	Valentine's Day
February 22	George Washington's Birthday
February (the third Monday)	Presidents' Day
May (the last Monday)	Memorial Day
July 4	Independence Day
September (the first Monday)	Labor Day
October 12 or (second Monday)	Columbus Day
October 31	Halloween
November (the fourth Thursday)	Thanksgiving Day
December 25	Christmas

PAIR PRACTICE   *Talk with another student. Use the list of holidays above.*

Student 1: When is .... ?
Student 2: It's in .... (month) ....

PAIR PRACTICE   *Talk with another student. Use the calendar.*

Student 1: When is …. (holiday) ………?
Student 2: It's on ………………

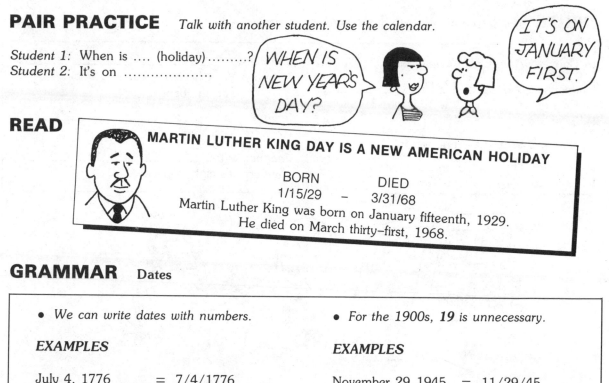

WHEN IS NEW YEAR'S DAY?

IT'S ON JANUARY FIRST.

READ

MARTIN LUTHER KING DAY IS A NEW AMERICAN HOLIDAY

BORN   DIED
1/15/29   –   3/31/68
Martin Luther King was born on January fifteenth, 1929.
He died on March thirty–first, 1968.

GRAMMAR   Dates

- *We can write dates with numbers.*

  EXAMPLES

  July 4, 1776   = 7/4/1776
  October 12, 1492 = 10/12/1492

- *For the 1900s, **19** is unnecessary.*

  EXAMPLES

  November 29, 1945 = 11/29/45

WRITE   *Show the dates below in words and numbers.*

AMERICAN PRESIDENTS	BORN	
George Washington	2/22/1732	*February 22, 1732*
Thomas Jefferson	4/13/1743	_____
Abraham Lincoln	2/12/1809	_____
Franklin Roosevelt	1/30/1882	_____
John Kennedy	5/29/1917	_____

CHALLENGE   *Write the dates of birth of three students in your class.*

NAME OF STUDENT   BIRTHDATE

1. _____   _____
2. _____   _____
3. _____   _____

WRITE *Fill in the blanks with a question or an answer.*

Caterer: Are you a new student?

Joanne: Yes, *I am.* _____

Caterer: Are you in the ESL class?

Joanne: No, _____

Caterer: What class are you in?

Joanne: I'm _____

Joanne: Is _____ ?

Caterer: Yes, this is my catering truck, and the bank's.

Joanne: Are _____ ?

Caterer: Yes, they're fifty cents.

Joanne: What _____ ?

Caterer: It's eight o'clock.

DICTATION *Cover the sentences under each line. Write the dictation, and then check your writing.*

Dear David,

1. _____
   Your address isn't in my roll book.

2. _____
   Tell me your address and telephone number.

3. _____
   Tell me your month, date, and year of birth, too.

4. _____
   Tell me at the break, OK?

5. _____
   Thank you.

Mr. Fuller

CHALLENGE   *Find the opposites, in the box, to the words below.*

1. quiet: _____

2. old: _____

3. new: _____

4. big: _____

5. dangerous: _____

6. dirty: _____

7. single: _____

8. strong: _____

safe	clean
weak	small
married	noisy
young	old

WORD ORDER   *Rewrite the questions in the correct word order. Then write your answer on the line below.*

QUESTIONNAIRE

1. name/What's/?/your *What's your name?* _____

Answer: _____

2. your/?/occupation/What's _____

Answer: _____

3. number/telephone/?/your/What's _____

Answer: _____

4. were/born/When/you/? _____

Answer: _____

5. are/old/How/you/? _____

Answer: _____

6. you/are/in/?/class/What _____

Answer: _____

7. room/your/?/What's/number _____

Answer: _____

8. teacher/?/your/Who's _____

Answer: _____

PHONICS   Short Vowels

LISTEN   *Pay attention to the vowel sounds. Then pronounce the words.*

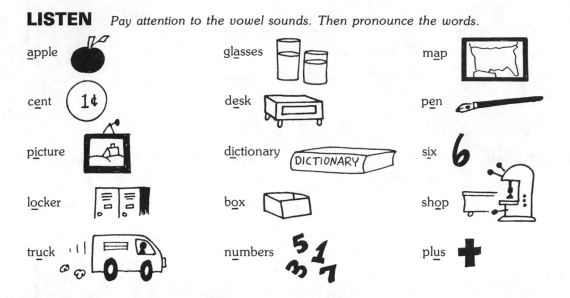

apple

cent   1¢

picture

locker

truck

glasses

desk

dictionary   DICTIONARY

box

numbers   5 1 3 7

map

pen

six   6

shop

plus

LISTEN   *Circle the word that has the same sound as the underlined letter in the first word.*

1. **glasses**	table	(class)	chalk
2. **picture**	six	light	five
3. **plus**	truck	four	you
4. **cent**	eat	men	one
5. **locker**	too	over	problem
6. **desk**	ten	thank	please
7. **box**	to	not	soda
8. **apples**	all	thank	say
9. **in**	I	widow	first
10. **number**	united	instructor	student

WRITE   *Fill in the words with a, e, i, o, or u.*

1. cl __a__ ss
2. b __i__ g
3. m____dern
4. J_____nuary

5. el_____ctrician
6. tr_____ck
7. M_____xico
8. F_____bruary

9. n____t
10. R_____ssia
11. th_____nks
12. Chr_____stmas

13. tw_____ns
14. pr_____blem
15. Nov_____mber
16. Th_____nksg____ving

Get Ready for a Dictation

COMPETENCIES	• Common Classroom Directions
	• Filling Out a Registration Card
	• Reading and Writing Addresses
GRAMMAR	• Imperative (*don't, let's*)
	• Definite Article
VOCABULARY	• Common Verbs
	• Classroom Words
PHONICS	• *sh* and *ch* Sounds

LISTEN

It's the beginning of class.

Mr. Barns: Hello, everybody!
Students: Hi!
Mr. Barns: Get ready for a dictation.
Students: A test?!
Mr. Barns: No, a dictation. Now, close your books.
Open your notebooks. Take a pen.
Listen to me carefully and write.
Wanda: Mr. Barns!
Mr. Barns: Yes, Wanda, what is it?
Wanda: Please speak slowly!

Mr. Barns: Please stand up and go to the chalkboard.
Miko: Who?
Mr. Barns: A volunteer.
Miko: Me!
Mr. Barns: OK. Pick up the chalk and write the dictation.
Miko: And then?
Mr. Barns: Then, go back to your seat and sit down.
Miko: Is this OK?
Mr. Barns: Students, look at the words on the chalkboard
and correct the mistakes.
Let's start at number one.

UNDERSTAND   *Circle **True** or **False**.*

1. The books are open for the dictation.	True	False
2. The students listen to Mr. Barns carefully.	True	False
3. Mr. Barns and the students write the dictation.	True	False
4. Miko is a volunteer.	True	False
5. "How's this?" means "Is this OK?"	True	False
6. The teacher and the students correct the mistakes.	True	False

WRITE   *Put the sentences in the correct order. Study the example below.*

___3___ Open it.

___1___ Stand up.

___4___ Come back.

___5___ Sit down.

___2___ Go to the door.

_____ Listen to the words.

_____ Let's correct the mistakes.

_____ Get ready for the dictation.

_____ Write the words.

_____ Open your notebooks.

_____ Pick up the chalk.

_____ Correct the mistakes.

_____ Go to the chalkboard.

_____ Write the dictation.

_____ Go back to your seat.

_____ Sit down.

_____ Go to the table.

_____ Stand up.

_____ Go back to your seat.

_____ Take a pen.

WRITE   *Choose the missing word, and then write it on the line.*

Pick
Open (1) *Open* your book.
Write

Help
Write (2)_____ a pen.
Take

Listen to
Look at (3)_____ the dictation.
Let's

Speak
Write (4)_____ the words.
Take

Correct
Pick up (5)_____ the mistakes.
Meet

Close
Stand (6)_____ your books.
Pick

Stand
Take (7)_____ up.
Pick

Meet
Speak (8)_____ to the door.
Go

Take
Open (9)_____ it.
Help

Meet
Speak (10)_____ the students "Good–bye."
Tell

See you all tomorrow. Bye.

PAIR PRACTICE
Talk with another student. Give directions to each other from the pictures in any logical order. Follow the directions.

EXAMPLE   Put a book on the table.
                    Open it.
                    Close it.

open   close   take   listen to   write

look at   read   put   stand up   go to

pick up   come   sit down   give   talk

CHALLENGE
Write a series of commands. Then give them to another student. He/she follows the commands.

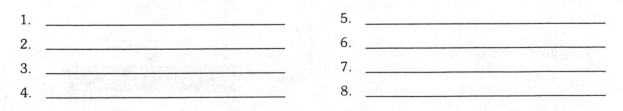

1. _____   5. _____
2. _____   6. _____
3. _____   7. _____
4. _____   8. _____

LISTEN

It's break time.

Mr. Barns:	Let's take a break!
Sami:	Good, I'm thirsty.
Maria:	Let's go to the catering truck.
Miko:	No, let's not go there.
Maria:	Why not?
Miko:	The food isn't very good.
Sami:	OK, let's go to the snack bar next door.
Maria:	Fine, let's go.

UNDERSTAND   *Circle **True** or **False**.*

1. It's break time.	True	False
2. Sami, Miko, and Maria are in the classroom.	True	False
3. The catering truck is next door.	True	False
4. Mr. Barns is thirsty.	True	False
5. The catering truck is the snack bar.	True	False

PAIR PRACTICE   *Talk with another student. Use the phrases below.*

Student 1: Come on. Let's ....
Student 2: No, let's not. Let's ....

1. meet at the catering truck/meet at the snack bar

2. go to the catering truck/go to the snack bar

3. stand up/sit down

4. walk/hurry up

5. hurry up/be careful

6. take a break/go home

LISTEN

After the break...

Mr. Barns: Sami, please do me a favor.
    Sami: Sure, what?
Mr. Barns: Go to the office and get me some chalk.
    Sami: Is that all?
Mr. Barns: No, wait! Get me some paper, too.
    Sami: OK.

Mr. Barns: Finished?
    Maria: No, not yet.
Mr. Barns: Leave it and do the exercise on the next page.
    Maria: What page?
Mr. Barns: Start here on page sixteen.
    Maria: All right.

    Sami: Oh! The bell.
Mr. Barns: Don't forget your homework.
  Students: Homework?!
Mr. Barns: Yes, the homework on page eighteen.
    Sami: Have a good weekend!
Mr. Barns: And you, too.

UNDERSTAND   *Circle **True** or **False**.*

1. Mr. Barns and Sami are in the office.	True	False
2. The chalk and the paper are in the office.	True	False
3. "Leave it" means "Stop."	True	False
4. "All right" means "OK."	True	False
5. The students have homework for the weekend.	True	False

WRITE   *Fill in the spaces with the words in the box.*

Joanne: Please, (1)_____*do*_____ me a favor.

David: Sure, what?

Joanne: (2)_____ to the ~~catering truck~~ dining room and

(3)_____ me some juice.

David: Is that all?

Joanne: No, it isn't. Please (4)_____ me some ~~potato~~ milk

~~chips~~, too. (5)_____ some money.

go	get
do	here's

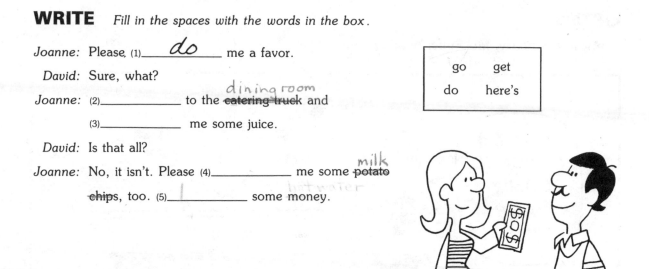

PAIR PRACTICE   *Talk with another student about the objects in the picture below.*

Student 1: Do me a favor.
Student 2: Sure, what?
Student 1: Please get me some ....
Student 2: What .... ?
Student 1: The .... over there.

LISTEN

The wood is heavy. Mr. Fuller needs help.

Mr. Fuller: Please give me a hand.
David: Sure.
Mr. Fuller: Pick it up.
David: OK.
Mr. Fuller: Now, be careful. Don't drop it.
David: Now what?
Mr. Fuller: Let's put it over there.
David: Is this OK?
Mr. Fuller: Hold it! Wait!
David: What's the matter?
Mr. Fuller: Turn it around.
David: How's this?
Mr. Fuller: Fine, now let's clean up and go home.
David: Great!

UNDERSTAND   *Circle **True** or **False**.*

1. David is careful.   True   False
2. The class is over.   True   False
3. "Hold it!" means "Stop!"   True   False
4. "What's the matter?" means "How's this?"   True   False
5. "Great!" means "Very good."   True   False

PAIR PRACTICE   *Talk with another student. Use the phrases below.*

Student 1: Hold it!
Student 2: What's the matter?
Student 1: Don't ....!

1. drop the glass
2. write on the desk
3. write on the walls
4. sit down
5. open the window

6. close the door
7. put it here
8. pick up the glass
9. forget your homework
10. ....

WRITE   *Help Wanda decide. Write* **Do it** *or* **Don't do it.**

1. Listen to the teacher.
2. Write on the walls.
3. Write on the desks.
4. Drop the glasses.
5. Take a break.
6. Correct your mistakes.
7. Be careful.
8. Do your homework.
9. Forget your books.
10. Go home.

Do it.
Don't do it.

PAIR PRACTICE

Talk with another student. Use the phrases below.

Student 1: Please ....
Student 2: Don't do / Do what?
Student 1: .... it ....

1. Turn the desk around.
2. Clean the room up.
3. Don't pick the glass up.

4. Fill this form out.
5. Don't turn the machine around.
6. Please give the pen back.

WRITE

Unscramble the letters.

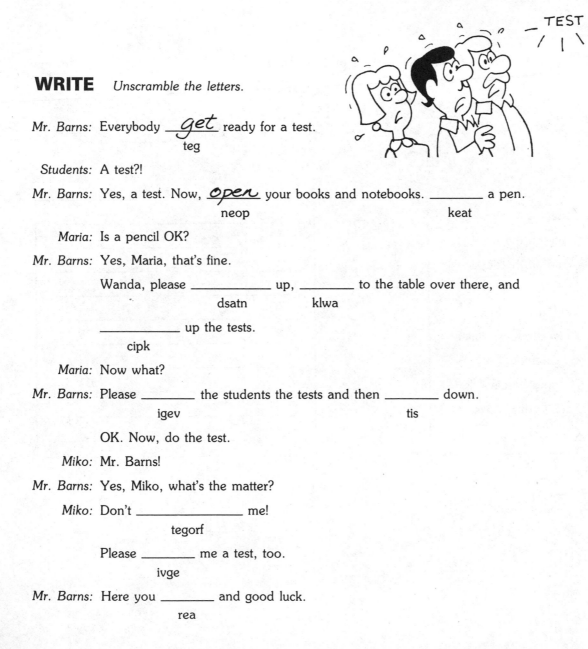

Mr. Barns: Everybody ___*get*___ ready for a test.
                              teg

Students: A test?!

Mr. Barns: Yes, a test. Now, ___*open*___ your books and notebooks. _____ a pen.
                                  neop   keat

Maria: Is a pencil OK?

Mr. Barns: Yes, Maria, that's fine.

Wanda, please _____ up, _____ to the table over there, and
                           dsatn   klwa

_____ up the tests.
        cipk

Maria: Now what?

Mr. Barns: Please _____ the students the tests and then _____ down.
                igev   tis

OK. Now, do the test.

Miko: Mr. Barns!

Mr. Barns: Yes, Miko, what's the matter?

Miko: Don't _____ me!
                  tegorf

Please _____ me a test, too.
             ivge

Mr. Barns: Here you _____ and good luck.
             rea

GRAMMAR The Definite Article *the*

	Singular			**Plural**		
Let's correct	**the**	dictation.	Let's correct	**the**	mistake	**s.**
Don't forget	**the**	pen!	Don't forget	**the**	pencil	**s.**
Please fill out	**the**	form.	Please fill out	**the**	card	**s.**

• *Use **the** in the singular and plural forms.*

WRITE   *Fill in the sentences with **the** and the name of the correct object to the right.*

1. Please give me <u>*the pencil*</u>
   over there.

2. Get me _____
   on the table.

3. Don't drop _____.

4. Let's go to _____.

WRITE   *Fill in the sentences with **the** and the names of the objects to the right.*

1. Put <u>*the book*</u> in <u>*the locker*</u>.

2. Take _____ from _____.

3. Don't drop _____ on _____.

4. Pick _____ up from _____.

LISTEN

Mona Boulos is in the counseling office. She wants to sign up for a class.

Mona: Is this the counseling office?
Counselor: Yes, it is.
Mona: Good, I want to register for a typing class.
Counselor: What level?
Mona: Beginning.
Counselor: Please fill out this form.
Use a pen. And please print.
Put your last name first.
Mona: All right.
Counselor: Then, give it back to me.
Mona: Here you are.
Counselor: Hold it. Wait a minute.
Mona: What's the matter?
Counselor: Your signature!
Please sign here.

I WANT TO REGISTER FOR A TYPING CLASS.

REGISTRATION CARD

NAME: *Boulos   Mona   —*
        last   first   middle
ADDRESS: *23   N. Shell St.   Apt.6*
      number   street   apartment
CITY: *Los Angeles* STATE: *CA* ZIP CODE: *90038*
DATE OF BIRTH: *11/29/29* NATIONALITY: *Lebanese*
CLASS: *Typing*   LEVEL: *Beginning*
TELEPHONE: *643-9821* SIGNATURE: *Mona Boulos*

Abbreviations:

St.   = street
Ave. = avenue
Blvd. = boulevard
Dr.   = drive
Rd.   = road
Apt. = apartment
#   = number (apt.)
N.   = north
S.   = south
E.   = east
W.   = west

UNDERSTAND   *Circle **True** or **False**.*

1. The new student is in the counseling office.	True	False
2. The woman is a beginning ESL student.	True	False
3. Her name is Mona.	True	False
4. Forms have lines.	True	False
5. "Fill out" means "write."	True	False
6. "Sign here" means "Please write your name here."	True	False

PAIR PRACTICE   *Ask and answer the questions for Mona.*

1. What's your first name?
2. What's your last name?
3. What's your address?
4. What's your zip code?
5. What's your telephone number?
6. What's your occupation?
7. What's your nationality?
8. What class are you in?
9. What level are you in?

IT'S...

IDENTIFICATION CARD

Name: *Mona Boulos*

Address: *23 N. Shell St., Apt. 6*
L.A. CA. 90038

Telephone: *643-9821*

Occupation: *artist*

Date of birth: *11/29/29*

Nationality: *Lebanese*

Class: *Typing*   Level: *Beginning*

PAIR PRACTICE   *Use the questions above. Talk about the identification cards below with another student.*

IDENTIFICATION CARD

Name: *David Fernandez*

Address: *13 Theater Dr.*
Los Angeles, CA 90088

Telephone: *421-9605*

Occupation: *Carpenter*

Date of Birth: *4/3/61*

Nationality: *American*

Class: *wood shop*   Level: *1*

IDENTIFICATION CARD

Name: *Sami Hamati*

Address: *2347 Third Blvd.*
Santa Monica, CA 92069

Telephone: *946-5210*

Occupation: *Auto Mechanic*

Date of Birth: *2/10/37*

Nationality: *Egyptian*

Class: *ESL*   Level: *ONE*

IDENTIFICATION CARD

Name: *Maria Corral*

Address: *396 Ship St.*
Santa Monica, CA 92069

Telephone: *787-6935*

Occupation: *Cashier*

Date of Birth: *4/3/1961*

Nationality: *Mexican*

Class: *ESL*   Level: *One*

IDENTIFICATION CARD

Name: *Paul Green*

Address: *23 S. Chain Ave.*
Los Angeles, CA 90048

Telephone: *253-7461*

Occupation: *Apartment Manager*

Date of Birth: *10/15/36*

Nationality: *American*

Class: *Wood shop*   Level: *one*

WRITE   *Fill out the registration card for Joanne Yates.*

REGISTRATION CARD

Name: <u>Joanne Yates</u>

Address: _____

_____

Telephone: _____   Occupation: _____

Date of birth: _____   Nationality: _____

Class: _____   Level:_____

Signature: _____

This is Joanne Yates.
She's a telephone operator.
She's from New York.
She's in the beginning wood shop class.
Her address is 65 Church Street, Apartment 3,
Los Angeles, California 90038.
Her telephone number is 643–0571.
Her date of birth is 3/13/55.

WRITE   *Fill out the registration card for yourself.*

REGISTRATION CARD

NAME: _____ first name ____ middle name

last name

ADDRESS: _____   apartment number

number   street name   ZIP CODE: _____

STATE: _____

CITY: _____   DATE OF BIRTH: __/__/__

TELEPHONE NUMBER: _____

SIGNATURE: _____

NATIONALITY: _____   LEVEL: _____

CLASS: _____

PAIR PRACTICE   *Fold this page. Look at only your side.*

Student 1

Listen to the questions and find the answers in the picture below.

Help your partner fill out an identification card for you. Tell your partner:

1. Your first name,
2. last name,
3. address,
4. city,
5. state,
6. zip code,
7. telephone number,
8. date of birth,
9. nationality,
10. class,
11. and level.

FOLD HERE

Student 2

Ask these questions.

1. Where are the people in the picture?
2. Are they all women?
3. Where are the women?
4. Where are the men?
5. Where are the lights?
6. Are the people careful? Why or why not?
7. What are the problems in the picture?
8. What's dangerous?
9. What's dirty?
10. What advice do you have for the people in the picture?

Fill in the identification card for your partner. Listen to the information.

```
IDENTIFICATION CARD

NAME: _____

ADDRESS: _____

_____

CITY: _____ STATE: _____

ZIP: _____

TELEPHONE: _____

DATE OF BIRTH: _____

NATIONALITY: _____

CLASS: _____

LEVEL: _____

SIGNATURE: _____
```

PAIR PRACTICE   *Talk with another student. Use **a** and **the**.*

Student 1: Please get me a ....
Student 2: What ....?
Student 1: The .... over there
in/on the ....

DICTATION   *Cover the sentences under each line. Write the dictation, then check your writing.*

Dear Roy,

1. _____
Please move the T.V.

2. _____
Put it on the table in the corner.

3. _____
Be careful. Don't drop it.

4. _____
Go and get Bobby.

5. _____
He's next door.

6. _____
See you at 6 o'clock.

7. _____
Thanks.
Nancy

WORD ORDER   *Write correct sentences with the words and phrases below.*

Dear Bobby,

1. *Please be home at 4 o'clock.*
   home
   at
   be
   4 o'clock.
   Please

2. _____
   your
   Don't
   homework.
   forget
   to do

3. _____
   up
   Clean
   room.
   your

4. _____
   Let's
   5 o'clock.
   at
   eat

5. _____
   Meet
   next
   door.
   me
   snack
   bar
   at
   the

6. _____
   you
   later,
   See
   bye.

Love,
Mom

PHONICS   *ch* and *sh*

LISTEN   *Pay attention to the underlined sound. Then pronounce the words.*

she

ca<u>sh</u>ier

<u>Ch</u>ain Road   <u>Ch</u>urch Street

a tea<u>ch</u>er

wat<u>ch</u>

LISTEN   *Circle the word that has the same sound as the underlined letters in the first word.*

1. **<u>sh</u>e**   chain   (ship)   they
2. **<u>ch</u>ain**   thirsty   church   snack
3. **<u>sh</u>ell**   show   see   change
4. **tea<u>ch</u>er**   machine   mechanic   watching
5. **Engli<u>sh</u>**   cash   match   six

WRITE   *Listen. Then fill in the blanks with* **sh** *or* **ch.**

1. __*Sh*__ e   5. wa_____   9. tea_____er
2. __*ch*__ air   6. _____alkboard 10. ca_____ier
3. _____ange   7. Engli_____   11. _____ip
4. wood _____op   8. _____inese   12. potato _____ips

Where Can I Get Some Shoes?

COMPETENCIES	• Understanding and Giving Simple Street Directions
	• Reading a Shopping Directory and a Schedule of Classes
	• Asking About a Job
GRAMMAR	• *can/can't*
	• Prepositions (*across from, next to, behind, between, near, in front of, to the right, to the left*)
VOCABULARY	• Store Names
	• Some Common Job Positions
	• Expressions of Time
	• Ordinal Numbers
	• Basic Shopping Terms
SPELLING	• Names of the Letters of the Alphabet
	• Alphabetization

READ

Wanda Bratko and Maria Corral are at a snack bar.

Maria: Let's go to the new Lincoln Shopping Center.
             Look! Here's an ad in the paper.
Wanda: What day is the shoe sale?
Maria: It's on the first and second.
Wanda: Oh, that's today! How can we get there?
Maria: It's not far. Come on. Let's walk.
Wanda: I can't. My feet hurt. I need new shoes.

LINCOLN SHOPPING CENTER			MONTHLY SALES SCHEDULE			
1st first Shoe Sale	2nd second Shoe Sale	3rd third Furniture Sale	4th fourth Furniture Sale	5th fifth Tool Sale	6th sixth Tool Sale	7th seventh Tool Sale
8th eigth Book Sale	9th ninth Book Sale	10th tenth Toy Sale	11th eleventh Toy Sale	12th twelfth Radio Sale	13th thirteenth Radio Sale	14th fourteenth T.V. Sale
15th fifteenth T.V. Sale	16th sixteenth Computer Sale	17th seventeenth Computer Sale	18th eighteenth Computer Sale	19th nineteenth Clothing Sale	20th twentieth Clothing Sale	21st twenty-first Clothing Sale
22nd twenty- second Department Store Sale	23rd twenty- third Department Store Sale	24th twenty- fourth Pet Sale	25th twenty- fifth Pet Sale	26th twenty- sixth Stationery Sale	27th twenty- seventh Stationery Sale	28th twenty- eighth Hardware Sale
29th twenty-ninth Hardware Sale	30th thirtieth Hardware Sale	31st thirty-first Hardware Sale				

UNDERSTAND   *Circle **True** or **False**.*

1. Today is the first or the second of the month.   True   False
2. "How can we get there?" means "How do we go there?"   True   False
3. The radio sale is from the fourteenth to the fifteenth.   True   False

PAIR PRACTICE   *Talk about the schedule above with another student.*

Student 1: What day is the .... sale?
Student 2: It's on the ....

READ

Wanda and Maria are now at the shopping center.

Wanda: This is a really nice place.
Maria: Yeah, and it's so big, too!
Wanda: How can we find the shoe store?
Maria: Let's look at the directory over there.
Wanda: What floor is the shoe store on?
Maria: It's upstairs on the second floor.
Wanda: Let's go.

LINCOLN SHOPPING CENTER DIRECTORY					
	Floor		Floor		Floor
Information Desk	1	Shoe Store	2	Women's Clothing	4
Drug Store	1	Hairdresser	3	Stationery Store	4
Department Store	1	Barber Shop	3	Restaurant	5
Lost and Found	1	Men's Clothing	3	Toy Store	5
Security Office	1	Children's Clothing	3	Radio and T.V. Store	5
Restrooms	1	Business Offices	3	Home Computer Store	5
Coffee Shop	2	Book Store	4	Pet Shop	5
Hardware Store	2	Movie Theaters	4		

PAIR PRACTICE   *Talk with another student about the directory above.*

Student 1:   What floor is/are the............... on?
Student 2:   It's/They're on the............... floor.

WHAT FLOOR ARE THE RESTROOMS ON?

THEY'RE ON THE FIRST FLOOR.

INFORMATION

READ   *Read the variations.*

WHAT FLOOR IS THE COFFEE SHOP ON?
WHERE'S THE HARDWARE STORE?
CAN YOU TELL ME WHERE THE BARBER SHOP IS?
WHAT FLOOR ARE THE MOVIE THEATERS ON?
WHERE ARE THE RESTAURANTS?
CAN YOU TELL ME WHERE THE RESTROOMS ARE?

INFORMATION

PAIR PRACTICE   *Practice the variations above with another student.*

Student 1:   ....?
Student 2:   It's/They're on the .... floor.

CAN YOU TELL ME WHERE THE OFFICES ARE?

THEY'RE ON THE THIRD FLOOR.

INFORMATION

READ

A shopper needs information.

FIFTH FLOOR Toy Store Radio and T.V. Store Pet Shop Home Computer Store Business Offices Restaurant	
	SECOND FLOOR Coffee Shop Shoe Store Furniture Store Hardware Store
FOURTH FLOOR Book Store Stationery Store Movie Theaters Women's Clothing	
	FIRST FLOOR Information Desk Bank Drug Store Department Store Restrooms Security Office
THIRD FLOOR Men's Clothing Hairdresser Barber Shop Children's Clothing	

Clerk: May I help you?
Shopper: Can you tell me where I can get some shoes?
Clerk: You can get shoes in the shoe store on the second floor.
Shopper: Thank you very much.

PAIR PRACTICE   *Talk with another student.*

Student 1: Where can I get ....?
Student 2: You can get .... in the ....

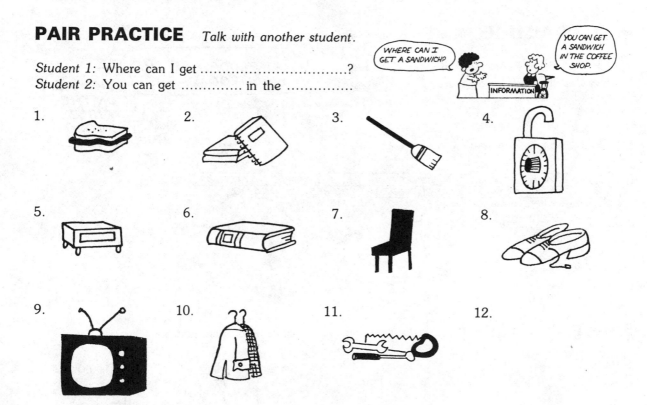

LISTEN

Maria asks a receptionist about a "Help Wanted" sign.

Maria asks a receptionist for an application.

Maria:	Excuse me. Can I have an application?
Receptionist:	Please speak to the manager in the personnel office.
Maria:	What room is she in?
Receptionist:	In Room 203. Go straight ahead down the hall.
Maria:	Thank you.

UNDERSTAND   *Circle **True** or **False**.*

1. The sign is in the window.	True	False
2. "Help Wanted" means "Jobs."	True	False
3. Wanda wants an application.	True	False
4. The personnel manager is a man.	True	False
5. The personnel office is in Room 203.	True	False
6. The personnel office is across the hall to the left.	True	False

READ

THE HOME COMPUTER COMPANY DIRECTORY

	Room		Room
President	201*	Accountant	306
Vice President	202	Receiving Department	307
Personnel Manager	203	Shipping Department	308
Secretary	204	Maintenance	
Receptionist	205	Department	109

PAIR PRACTICE   *Talk to another student about the directory above.*

Student 1:   What room is the .... in?
Student 2:   In Room ....

> WHAT ROOM IS THE SECRETARY IN?

> IN ROOM TWO·OH·FOUR.

READ

> HOW CAN I GET TO .... ?

> GO STRAIGHT AHEAD.

> GO DOWN THE HALL TO THE LEFT.

> GO DOWN THE HALL TO THE RIGHT.

> GO ACROSS THE HALL.

> GO DOWNSTAIRS.

> GO UPSTAIRS.

201   203

SECOND FLOOR
208–209

204   202

PAIR PRACTICE   *Talk to another student about the picture above.*

Student 1: How can I get to ....?
Student 2: Go ....

> HOW CAN I GET TO ROOM 205?

> GO DOWN THE HALL TO THE LEFT.

---

* 1. The first number of the room shows the floor. Example: Room **2**01 is on the second floor.
    2. The first floor = the ground floor.

LISTEN

Maria is in the personnel office.

Manager: May I help you?
Maria: Can I speak to the personnel manager?
Manager: I'm the manager. Is it about the "Help Wanted" sign in the window?
Maria: Yes, it is.
Manager: Can you fix electronic equipment?
Maria: No, I can't. I'm a cashier.
Manager: I'm sorry, but we need a technician, not a cashier.
Maria: Oh! I see. Sorry to bother you.
Manager: I'm sorry I can't help you.
Maria: That's OK.

UNDERSTAND   *Circle **True** or **False**.*

1. Wanda can fix electronic equipment.   True   False
2. The personnel manager is a technician.   True   False
3. Maria is a cashier.   True   False
4. "I see" means "I understand."   True   False
5. The personnel manager is sorry to bother Wanda.   True   False

CHALLENGE   *Underline the words **can** and **can't** in the sentences above.*

GRAMMAR   *can*

Questions	*Affirmative*	*Negative*
Can you fix this?	Yes, I **can** fix it.	No, I **can't** fix it.

● *We often pronounce* **can** *as* /kn/ *in speech, except in short answers.*

PAIR PRACTICE   *Talk with another student. Use the pictures below.*

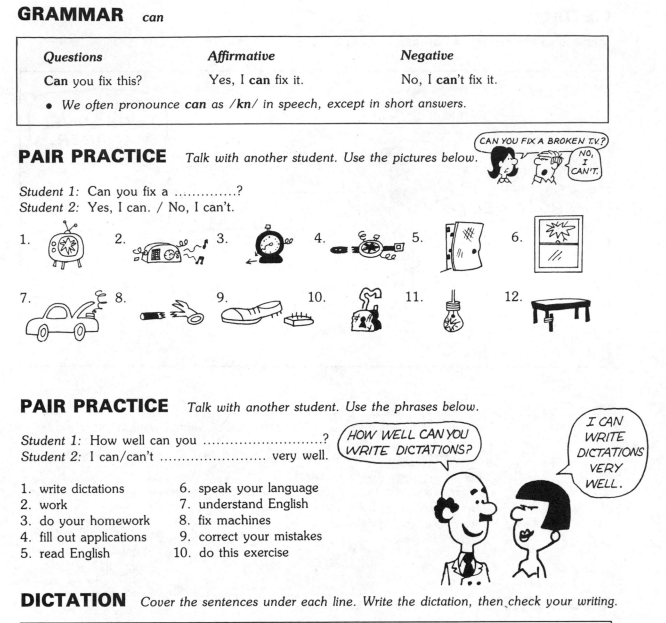

CAN YOU FIX A BROKEN T.V.?

NO, I CAN'T.

Student 1: Can you fix a ....?
Student 2: Yes, I can. / No, I can't.

1.   2.   3.   4.   5.   6.

7.   8.   9.   10.   11.   12.

PAIR PRACTICE   *Talk with another student. Use the phrases below.*

Student 1: How well can you ....?
Student 2: I can/can't .... very well.

1. write dictations
2. work
3. do your homework
4. fill out applications
5. read English

6. speak your language
7. understand English
8. fix machines
9. correct your mistakes
10. do this exercise

HOW WELL CAN YOU WRITE DICTATIONS?

I CAN WRITE DICTATIONS VERY WELL.

DICTATION   *Cover the sentences under each line. Write the dictation, then check your writing.*

Dear Stephen,

1. _____
   I'm sorry to bother you.

2. _____
   Can you help me?

3. _____
   My shoe is broken.

4. _____
   I can't fix it.

5. _____
   Can you fix it?

6. _____
   See you in class at 7 o'clock.

Wanda

LISTEN

Maria and Wanda are at the shoe store.

Wanda: Well, here we are.
Maria: Look at all the shoes.
Wanda: I like those black shoes.
Maria: Where?
Wanda: Next to the red shoes.
Maria: Oh, between the red shoes and the brown shoes?
Wanda: No, behind the blue boots.
Maria: Oh, yes, they're nice.

Salesman: May I help you?
Wanda: Can I try on the black shoes over there?
Salesman: Can you show me?
Wanda: There! Those shoes in front of the white tennis shoes.
Salesman: These shoes?
Wanda: Yes, those are the shoes.

An hour later...

Salesman: How are they?
Wanda: They fit fine.
Salesman: Is that all?
Wanda: Yes, I think so.
Salesman: Please pay the cashier over there, and come back again.
Wanda: Thank you.

UNDERSTAND   *Circle **True** or **False**.*

1. Wanda wants red shoes.	True	False
2. The black shoes are between the red and brown shoes.	True	False
3. The shoes fit fine.	True	False
4. The salesperson is a woman.	True	False
5. The cashier is near the salesperson.	True	False

READ

The coffee cup is **next to** the box.
The pencil is **behind** the note pad.
The lock and key are **in front of** the glasses.
The note pad is **between** the dictionary and the glasses.

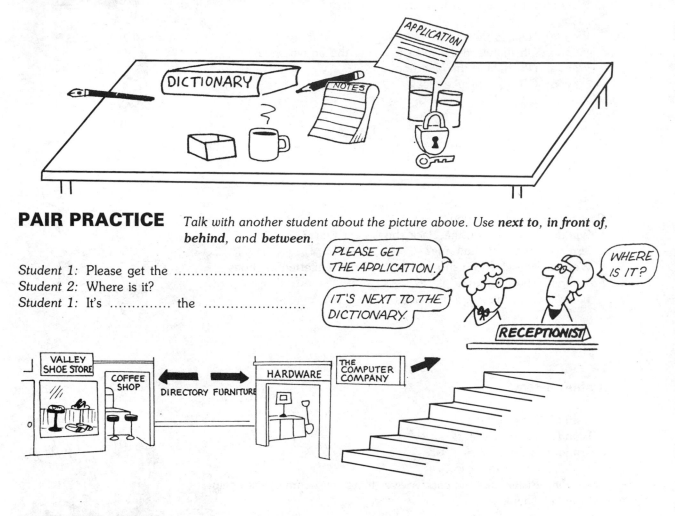

PAIR PRACTICE

*Talk with another student about the picture above. Use **next to**, **in front of**, **behind**, and **between**.*

Student 1: Please get the ....
Student 2: Where is it?
Student 1: It's .... the ....

PAIR PRACTICE

*Use **across from**, **down the hall**, **to the right**, **to the left**, **downstairs**, and **upstairs**. Talk with another student about the picture above.*

Student 1: Excuse me. Where's the .... ?
Student 2: It's ....

LISTEN

Wanda and Maria meet Sami at school.

Sami: Hi, Wanda. Are those new shoes?
Wanda: Uh–huh.
Sami: They're nice.
Wanda: Thanks.
Maria: Sami. What's that in your hand?
Sami: A schedule of classes.
Maria: Where can I get one?
Sami: In the main office.
Maria: What floor is it on?
Sami: On the first floor.
Maria: What room is it in?
Sami: In Room 105, I think.
Go downstairs, and then turn right.
It's around the corner.
Maria: Thanks.

UNDERSTAND   *Circle True or False.*

1. Wanda, Maria, and Sami are at the shopping center.   True   False
2. They are on the second floor.   True   False
3. Sami wants a schedule of classes.   True   False
4. The schedules of classes are in the main office.   True   False
5. The main office is downstairs.   True   False
6. The schedules of classes are near the door.   True   False

READ

SCHEDULE OF CLASSES				

Directory

Principal	101		Main Office	103
Vice Principal	102		Counselor	104

Class	Level	Room	Time	Teacher
Typing	1	109	6:30-9:30	Mr. Brown
Typing	2	110	6:30-9:30	Mrs. Gold
Wood Shop	1-2	206	6:30-9:30	Mr. Fuller
English as a Second Language	1	123	2:30-5:00	Ms. Childs
English as a Second Language	1	204	7:00-9:30	Mr. Barns
English as a Second Language	2	315	2:30-5:00	Mrs. Green
English as a Second Language	2	210	7:00-9:30	Mr. Thompson
English as a Second Language	3	303	7:00-9:30	Mrs. Woodman

PAIR PRACTICE   *Talk with another student about the schedule of classes above.*

Student 1: What room is the .... class in?

or

What floor is the .... class on?

or

What time is the .... class?

or

Who's the .... teacher?

Student 2: It's ....

DICTATION   *Cover the sentences under each line. Write the dictation, and then check your writing.*

Sam,

1. _____

Can you help me?

2. _____

I need a schedule of classes.

3. _____

Where can I get one?

4. _____

You can tell me at the break.

5. _____

Meet me near the door. OK?

Mibo

CHALLENGE   *Go to the main office of your school, ask for a schedule of classes, bring it to class, and show the students.*

READ AND DRAW   *Finish drawing the picture. Follow the directions below.*

1. Draw a catering truck to the right of the adult school.
2. Draw a tree behind the catering truck.
3. Draw a table in front of the catering truck.
4. Draw some people around the table.
5. Draw a snack bar across the street from the school.
6. Draw a store next to the snack bar.
7. Draw a fence between the snack bar and the store.
8. Draw a "Help Wanted" sign in the store window.
9. Draw some clouds over the buildings.
10. Draw a few cars on the street.
11. Draw ....

PAIR PRACTICE   *Fold this page. Look at only your side.*

Student 1	**Student 2**

Student 1

Listen to the questions and find the answers in the Schedule of Classes below.

SCHEDULE OF CLASSES			
Class	Room	Time	Teacher
ESL 1	123	2:30	Ms. Childs
ESL 2	210	7:00	Mr. Thompson
ESL 3	303	7:00	Mrs. Woodman
Auto Mechanics	130	6:30	Mr. West
French 1	207	7:00	Ms. Blanche
Spanish 1	301	7:00	Mr. Gonzalez

Student 2

Ask these questions.

1. What room is the French class in?
2. What floor is the auto mechanics class on?
3. Who's the ESL 1 teacher?
4. What time is the Spanish class?
5. What room is ESL 1 in?
6. What floor is ESL 2 on?
7. What time is the ESL 3 class?
8. Who is the French teacher?

FOLD HERE

Now ask these questions.

1. What room is the secretary in?
2. What floor is the bookkeeper on?
3. Who's in Room 101?
4. What room is the Main Office?
5. What floor is the Counseling Office on?
6. Who's in Room 202?

Now listen to the questions and find the answers in the school directory below.

FOLD HERE

SCHOOL DIRECTORY	
	Room
Principal	101
Vice Principal	102
Main Office	103
Secretary	103
Bookkeeper	208
Counseling Office	104
Maintenance	306
Nurse	202

LISTEN   *Names of the letters of the alphabet.*

THE ALPHABET: A B C D E F G H I J K L M N O P Q R S T U V W X Y Z

EXCUSE ME, MIKO, PLEASE SPELL YOUR LAST NAME.

T-A-K-A-H-A-S-H-I.

PLEASE SPELL YOUR FIRST NAME, TOO.

M-I-K-O.

READ   *Spell the students' names in the roll books.*

WOOD SHOP ROLL BOOK

Last Name	First Name
Green,	Paul
Landry,	Rita
Yates,	Joanne
Monte,	Raymond
Monte,	Roberto

ESL ROLL BOOK

Last Name	First Name
Corral,	Mario
Corral,	Maria
Chu,	Li
Chu,	Yen
Bratko,	Wanda
Bratko,	Stephen
Hamati,	Sami
Takahashi,	Miko

PAIR PRACTICE   *Talk with another student.*

Student 1: Please spell your first name.
Student 2: ....
Student 1: Now spell your last name.
Student 2: ....

PLEASE SPELL YOUR FIRST NAME.

NOW SPELL YOUR LAST NAME.

M-A-R-I-A.

C-O-R-R-A-L.

WRITE   *Help the teachers put the names from the lists above in alphabetical order.*

WOOD SHOP ROLL BOOK

Last Name	First Name

ESL ROLL BOOK

Last Name	First Name

CHALLENGE   *Alphabetize the Lincoln Shopping Center Directory.*

LINCOLN SHOPPING CENTER DIRECTORY

	Floor		Floor		Floor
Information Desk	1	Shoe Store	2	Women's Clothing	4
Drug Store	1	Business Offices	2	Stationery Store	4
Department Store	1	Hairdresser	3	Restaurant	5
Lost and Found	1	Barber Shop	3	Toy Store	5
Security Office	1	Men's Clothing	3	Radio and T.V. Store	5
Restrooms	1	Children's Clothing	3	Home Computer Store	5
Coffee Shop	2	Book Store	4	Pet Shop	5
Hardware Store	2	Movie Theaters	4		

LINCOLN SHOPPING CENTER DIRECTORY

FLOOR   FLOOR

1. *Barber Shop*   *3*   13. _____ _____

2. _____ _____   14. _____ _____

3. _____ _____   15. _____ _____

4. _____ _____   16. _____ _____

5. _____ _____   17. _____ _____

6. _____ _____   18. _____ _____

7. _____ _____   19. _____ _____

8. _____ _____   20. _____ _____

9. _____ _____   21. _____ _____

10. _____ _____   22. _____ _____

11. _____ _____   23. _____ _____

12. _____ _____

CHALLENGE   *List six stores near your house in alphabetical order.*

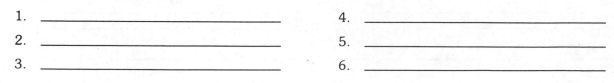

1. _____   4. _____

2. _____   5. _____

3. _____   6. _____

Let's Have a Party

COMPETENCIES	• Making a Work Schedule
	• Describing Household Chores
GRAMMAR	• The Present Habitual Tense *(do/don't)*
	• Using Expressions of Time
VOCABULARY	• Names for Parts of the Day, Days, and Months
	• Common Action Verbs
	• Common Household Items
SPELLING	• Noun Plurals
CAPITALIZATION	• Names, Places, Days, Months
	• Beginning of Sentences, and the Pronoun *I*

READ

It's evening. Roy and Nancy Barns are at home.

Roy: Let's have a party.
       We can invite the students from school.
Nancy: When?
Roy: What about next weekend?
Nancy: What day?
Roy: Next Saturday evening?
Nancy: OK, but think about all the work before a party.
Roy: I can help you with the work.
Nancy: What do you mean, "You can help me"?
Roy: We can share the work.
Nancy: Let's talk about it tomorrow, all right?
Roy: OK. Now let's go to sleep.

UNDERSTAND   *Circle **True** or **False**.*

1. Saturday is on the weekend.	True	False
2. The party is on Sunday evening.	True	False
3. Roy wants to invite the students to the party.	True	False
4. The work is for the party.	True	False
5. Roy is tired.	True	False

READ

A note from Nancy.

Friday

Dear Roy,

Here's my check list for the party. What can you do today? I can do the rest tonight. See you this afternoon.

1. vacuum the carpet
2. replace the light bulb in the hall
3. fix the toilet
4. go shopping for food
5. make ice cubes
6. clean the bathroom
7. wash the glasses and dishes
8. sweep the kitchen floor
9. set the table
10. arrange the flowers
11. move the furniture

12. iron the tablecloth
13. water the plants
14. dust the furniture
15. choose the music
16. invite the neighbors

Love,
Nancy

ISN'T A PARTY FUN?

WRITE   *Divide the work for Nancy and Roy.*

Roy	Nancy
1. _____	1. _____
2. _____	2. _____
3. _____	3. _____
4. _____	4. _____
5. _____	5. _____
6. _____	6. _____
7. _____	7. _____
8. _____	8. _____

READ

Roy and Nancy are on the telephone.

Roy: Hello.
Nancy: Hi, Roy, do you have my note?
Roy: Yes, but I can't get ready for the party today. I'm really busy.
Nancy: Well, I'm really busy, too.
Roy: Can't we get ready tomorrow?
Nancy: Isn't that late?
Roy: I know, but then we can do the work together.
Nancy: OK. You make a work schedule for tomorrow.
Roy: Sure. See you tonight. Bye.
Nancy: Bye.

WRITE   *Make a work schedule for Roy and Nancy.*

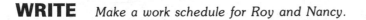

PARTY WORK SCHEDULE

	Morning	**Afternoon**	**Evening**
First:			
Second:			
Third:			
Fourth:			
Fifth:			

Then let's take a shower and get dressed. Let's leave some time to sit down and relax before the party, ok?

Love, Roy

UNDERSTAND   *Circle **True** or **False**.*

1. Roy and Nancy aren't very busy today.   True   False
2. Today is Thursday.   True   False
3. Tomorrow is Saturday.   True   False
4. The work schedule is for today.   True   False
5. Roy wants to relax before the party.   True   False

GRAMMAR   Present Habitual Tense

• Use the present habitual tense for all regular or habitual acts.	• Use **do** for questions in the present habitual with **I**, **you**, **we**, and **they**.
EXAMPLES	*EXAMPLES*

I	**wash**	my clothes on Saturday.
I	**have**	your note.
You	**make**	a work schedule.

	Do	you have my note?
What	**do**	you do in the morning?

GRAMMAR   Prepositions of Time: *on* and *in*

• Use the preposition **on** before days.	• Use the preposition **in** before months.
EXAMPLES	*EXCEPTIONS*

on	Friday
in	January

in	the morning	**in**	the evening
in	the afternoon	**at**	night

READ   *Make complete sentences with the words in the box below.*

	wash	my homework	in the evening.
	make	flowers	in the afternoon.
I	do	the floors	on Saturday.
You	see	dinner	in May.
We	sweep	shopping	on the weekend.
They	iron	my clothes	on Friday.
	clean		in the morning.

READ   *Make questions with the words in the box below. Then answer them.*

	work	on Saturday?
	go shopping	on Sunday?
Do you	have parties	in December?
	clean the house	in June?
	go to the park	on Friday?

PAIR PRACTICE   *Talk with another student. Answer in your own words.*

Student 1:   What do you do ....?
Student 2:   I ....

1. in the morning	3. in the evening	5. every day	7. on Friday	9. on the weekend
2. in the afternoon	4. before a party	6. after a party	8. on Saturday	10. ....

PAIR PRACTICE   *Talk with another student. Answer in your own words.*

Student 1: When do you ....?
Student 2: I ....

1. have free time
2. go shopping for food
3. clean the house
4. have parties
5. wash your clothes

6. work
7. do your homework
8. make dinner
9. have dinner
10. ....

WHEN DO YOU HAVE FREE TIME?

I HAVE FREE TIME ON SATURDAY.

PAIR PRACTICE   *Talk with another student. Answer in your own words.*

Student 1: Where do you .... ?
Student 2: I ....

1. have lunch
2. live
3. study
4. go to school
5. buy clothes

6. wash your clothes
7. work
8. go shopping
9. do your homework
10. ....

WHERE DO YOU HAVE LUNCH?

I HAVE LUNCH AT WORK.

WRITE   *Write your schedule. Complete the sentences with some of the time expressions in the box below.*

on Monday	on Tuesday	on Wednesday	on Thursday
on Friday	on Saturday	on Sunday	on the weekend
in the morning	in the afternoon	in the evening	every day

MY WEEKLY SCHEDULE

1. I wash my clothes _____

2. I go shopping for food _____

3. I dust the furniture _____

4. I vacuum the carpets _____

5. I sweep the floor _____

6. I iron clothes _____

7. I do my homework _____

8. I make dinner _____

READ

Sami and Miko are at the party.

Nancy: Here they come!
  Roy: Hi, Sami. Hi, Miko.
         This is my wife, Nancy.
 Miko: Pleased to meet you, Mrs. Barns.
 Sami: Pleased to meet you, too.
Nancy: Let me introduce you to the guests.

UNDERSTAND   *Circle **True** or **False**.*

1. Sami and Miko are guests.	True	False
2. Roy and Nancy are guests, too.	True	False
3. "What do you do?" means "What's your profession?"	True	False
4. "Not far" means "near."	True	False
5. Computers are machines.	True	False

WRITE   *Underline the word **do** in all the sentences above.*

PAIR PRACTICE   *Talk with another student. Use the phrases below.*

Student 1: When do you ....?
Student 2: I .... on ....
            What about you?
Student 2: On ....

1. write letters
2. call your friends
3. go shopping for food

4. wash your clothes
5. clean the house
6. visit your neighbors

7. relax
8. work
9. ....

PAIR PRACTICE   *Talk with another student. Use the phrases below.*

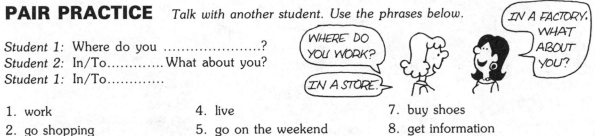

Student 1: Where do you ....?
Student 2: In/To.............What about you?
Student 1: In/To.............

1. work
2. go shopping
3. go on vacation

4. live
5. go on the weekend
6. meet people

7. buy shoes
8. get information
9. ....

WRITE   *Fill in the spaces with the words in the box.*

can	can't	do	'm	is

Roy: __Do__ you have a minute?

Nancy: Yeah, sure, what _____ it?

Roy: _____ you go shopping with me?

Nancy: I _____ go right now. I _____ busy.

Roy: When _____ you have time?

Nancy: After work. _____ you meet me here?

Roy: That sounds fine. See you at work at five.

Nancy: OK. See you then.

READ

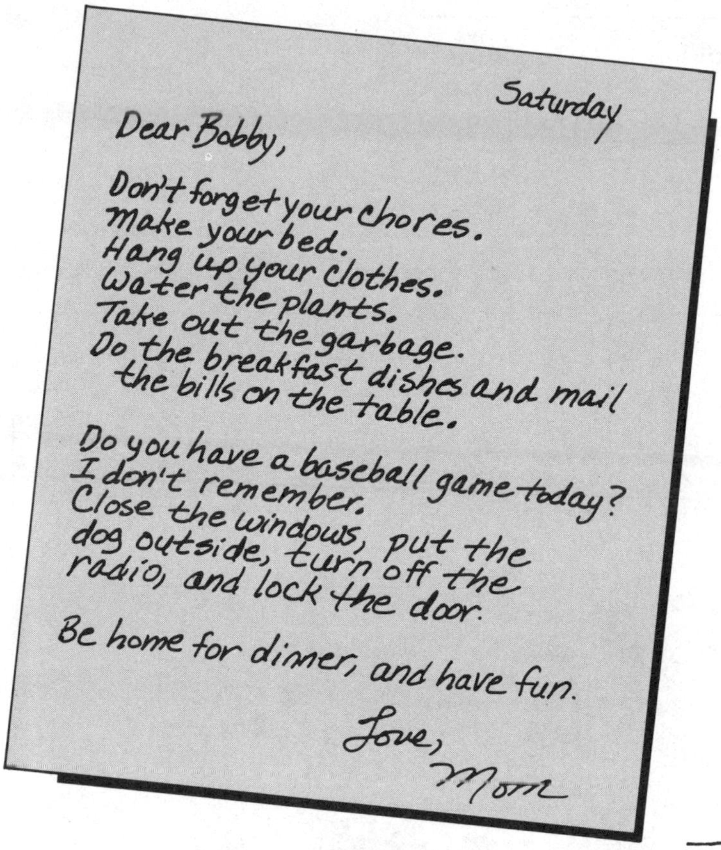

Saturday

Dear Bobby,

Don't forget your chores.
Make your bed.
Hang up your clothes.
Water the plants.
Take out the garbage.
Do the breakfast dishes and mail
the bills on the table.

Do you have a baseball game today?
I don't remember.
Close the windows, put the
dog outside, turn off the
radio, and lock the door.

Be home for dinner, and have fun.

Love,
Mom

WRITE   *Organize Bobby's chores.*

First, _____

Second, _____

Third, _____

Fourth, _____

Fifth, _____

Sixth, _____

Seventh, _____

Eighth, _____

Ninth, _____

Tenth, _____

UNDERSTAND   *Circle **True** or **False**.*

1.	It's the weekend.	True	False
2.	The baseball game is today.	True	False
3.	Mother's at home.	True	False
4.	It's Saturday morning.	True	False
5.	The windows are open.	True	False

GRAMMAR   Short Answers: Present Habitual

Question	Affirmative	Negative
Do you ....?	Yes, I do.	No, I don't.

PAIR PRACTICE   Ask and answer the questions with another student. Use the short answers.

1. Do you do chores at home?
2. Do you like to do chores?
3. Do you take out the garbage?
4. Do you make your bed?
5. Do you wash your clothes?
6. Do you ....?

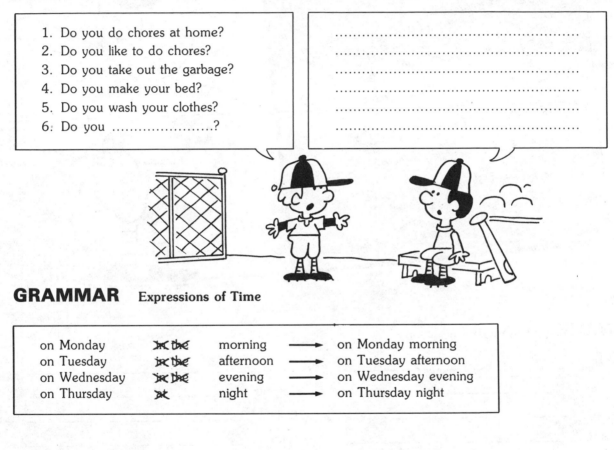

GRAMMAR   Expressions of Time

on Monday	~~in the~~	morning	⟶	on Monday morning
on Tuesday	~~in the~~	afternoon	⟶	on Tuesday afternoon
on Wednesday	~~in the~~	evening	⟶	on Wednesday evening
on Thursday	~~at~~	night	⟶	on Thursday night

PAIR PRACTICE   Talk with another student. Use the phrases below.

Student 1: When do you ....?
Student 2: On ....
            What about you?
Student 1: On ....

1. water the plants
2. go to school
3. go to the movies
4. go shopping for food

5. clean the house
6. do your chores
7. pay your bills
8. buy clothes

WRITE   *Fill in your weekly schedule.*

MY WEEKLY SCHEDULE

DATES: From: _____

(Month, Date, Year)

To: _____

(Month, Date, Year)

Monday

Morning: _____

_____

Afternoon: _____

_____

Evening: _____

_____

Tuesday

Morning: _____

_____

Afternoon: _____

_____

Evening: _____

_____

Wednesday

Morning: _____

_____

Afternoon: _____

_____

Evening: _____

_____

Thursday

Morning: _____

_____

Afternoon: _____

_____

Evening: _____

_____

Friday

Morning: _____

_____

Afternoon: _____

_____

Evening: _____

_____

Saturday

Morning: _____

_____

Afternoon: _____

_____

Evening: _____

_____

Sunday

Morning: _____

_____

Afternoon: _____

_____

Evening: _____

_____

WRITE   *Make a list of duties for your family members.*

WRITE   *Answer Bobby's mother's note. Use the words in the box below.*

don't	do	are
can't	's	'm

Dear Mom,

The dog ___'s___ outside, and my chores _____ finished. I _____ at the park with my friends. Where _____ my new tennis shoes? _____ you know? I _____ remember! I _____ find the shoes. Please _____ forget my favorite dessert for dinner. See you about 4:30.

Love, Bobby

PAIR PRACTICE   *Fold the page in half. Look at your side only.*

Student 1	Student 2

Student 1

Your partner tells you his or her schedule. You write it.

Appointment Book

Sunday: _____

Monday: _____

Tuesday: _____

Wednesday: _____

Thursday: _____

Friday: _____

Saturday: _____

Now, you tell your partner your daily schedule. Your partner writes your schedule in the appointment book.

What do you do ....?

at 8 a.m.

at 10 a.m.

at 12 noon

at 2 p.m.

at 4 p.m.

at 6 p.m.

at 8 p.m.

at 10 p.m.

Student 2

Tell your partner your daily schedule. Your partner writes the schedule in the appointment book.

What do you do ....?

on Sundays

on Mondays

on Tuesdays

on Wednesdays

on Thursdays

on Fridays

on Saturdays

FOLD HERE

Now, your partner tells you his or her schedule. You write it in the appointment book.

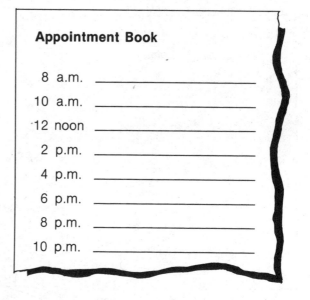

Appointment Book

8 a.m. _____

10 a.m. _____

12 noon _____

2 p.m. _____

4 p.m. _____

6 p.m. _____

8 p.m. _____

10 p.m. _____

FOLD HERE

SPELLING Noun Plurals

- *Add −s to most words.*

EXAMPLE

one pencil
two pencils

- *Add es to words with s, sh, ch, z, ch, or x at the end.*

EXAMPLES

one dress   three dresses
one box   five boxes
one dish   four dishes

- *For a word with y at the end after a consonant, change the y to i and add −es.*

EXAMPLE

one city   two cities

- *For a word with y at the end after a vowel, add only −s.*

EXAMPLE

one day   seven days

Irregular forms

a man/two men   a child/three children
a woman/two women   a person/people

WRITE *Change the words under the lines to the plural.*

Write a note to Mario.

1. Put on your _____.
            glass

2. Open the _____.
            box

3. Take out the _____.
            watch

4. Put on these _____.
            pant

5. Give it to the _____.
            person

6. Ask those _____ and _____.
         man   woman

LA ____
ROOM

Tell the _____ to finish
           child

their _____ and the _____.
      exercise   chore

Please wash the _____ and please
               dish

bring my _____ to school.
         book

My homework is two _____ late!
            day

Love, Maria

SPELLING   Capitalization

- *We use capitals (big letters) for names of people, places, days, and months.*

EXAMPLES

People: Roy Barns   Days: Monday
         Mr. Monte   New Year's Day
         Miko   Christmas

Places: New York   Months: January
         63 Main Street   February
         The Home Computer Store   November

- *We use a capital at the beginning of every sentence.*

EXAMPLE

Put on your glasses.

- *Always capitalize the pronoun **I**.*

EXAMPLE

My friends and I are at the park.

WRITE   *Capitalize the letters in the dialogs below when necessary.*

What do you do every week?

on mondays, i go to work early. on tuesdays, i watch my favorite program on television. i wash my clothes on wednesdays, and I call my parents in new york every thursday evening. on fridays, i go to carl's market for food. i clean the house on saturdays, and i try to rest on sundays.

CHALLENGE   *Write the names, addresses, and birthdates of three people in your class. Be sure to capitalize the names, street names, and months.*

	NAME	ADDRESS	BIRTHDATE
1.	_____	_____	_____
2.	_____	_____	_____
3.	_____	_____	_____

6

A Typical Day

COMPETENCIES	• Talking About Daily Activities
	• Writing a Simple Letter
	• Addressing an Envelope
GRAMMAR	• The Present Habitual Tense (*–s, does, doesn't*)
	• Object Pronouns
	• Verb + Infinitive
VOCABULARY	• Verbs Used in Daily Activities
PHONICS	• The Long *a* Sound (as in *mail*)

READ

A letter from Joanne.

Dear Mom and Dad,

I'm in my new apartment now, and I like it very much. I live near my job at the telephone company and the local adult school. Now I can sleep later in the morning. I leave my apartment at 7:45 and walk to work. It's only a five-minute walk. I punch in at 8 a.m.

I have a new position at work. I'm an operator. I speak to people all day. I give them information and help them with long distance calls. I eat lunch at noon with a new friend. (He's an employee, too.) I leave work at 5 p.m. and go straight home. I eat dinner and get ready for school. My wood shop class is interesting and my teacher is very helpful. It's time for school. Write soon.

Love,
Joanne

P.S. Please come to visit me. You can see my new place, and maybe meet my new friend.

UNDERSTAND   *Circle True, False, or I don't know.*

1.	Joanne lives in a new apartment.	True	False	I don't know.
2.	Joanne lives in a new building.	True	False	I don't know.
3.	Joanne works at a new job.	True	False	I don't know.
4.	Joanne takes the bus to work.	True	False	I don't know.
5.	The wood shop class meets in the evening.	True	False	I don't know.
6.	Joanne likes her teacher.	True	False	I don't know.

GRAMMAR   Third Person Singular Endings of the Present Habitual Tense

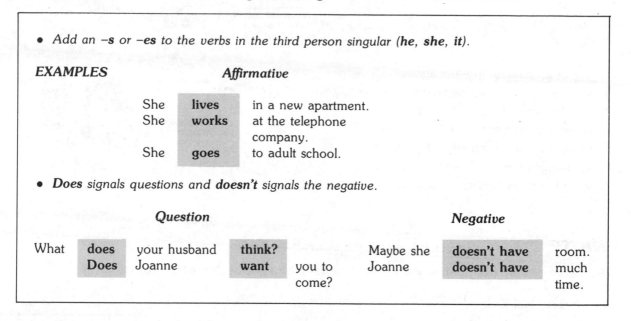

• *Add an* **–s** *or* **–es** *to the verbs in the third person singular (**he, she, it**).*

EXAMPLES   *Affirmative*

She   **lives**   in a new apartment.
She   **works**   at the telephone company.
She   **goes**   to adult school.

• ***Does*** *signals questions and **doesn't** signals the negative.*

Question

What   **does**   your husband   **think?**
       Does   Joanne   **want**   you to come?

Negative

Maybe she   **doesn't have**   room.
Joanne   **doesn't have**   much time.

WRITE   *Underline all the verbs in the third person singular.*

Clara Yates is on the telephone with her friend, Mabel.

Clara: Hello, Mabel? This is Clara.
Mabel: Hi, Clara, how are you?
Clara: Fine. I have a letter from Joanne.
Mabel: Oh, really? What does she say?
Clara: She lives in a new apartment and she likes it very much. She lives near her job and school. She writes about her job, too. She likes it very much. She works for the telephone company, you know. She says it's a very interesting job. She's a very busy person. She works all day, and then goes to an adult school in the evening. She takes a wood shop class. She wants me to come and visit her next month. What do you think? Is it a good idea?
Mabel: I don't know. What does your husband think?
Clara: He wants to go.
Mabel: Don't you want to go, too?
Clara: Maybe Joanne doesn't have room for us.
Mabel: But she wants you to come!
Clara: Yes, she does.
Mabel: Then, go!

PAIR PRACTICE   *Talk with another student. Use the phrases below.*

Student 1: Does Joanne .... or..............?
Student 2: She .... s ....

1. live in a house or in an apartment
2. work at school or at the telephone company
3. give information or get information
4. leave the apartment at 7:30 or 8:30
5. go to work or to school in the evening
6. eat breakfast or lunch with her friends
7. want her parents to visit this month or next month

WRITE   *Fill in the spaces below with the words from the box.*

Mr. Yates comes home after work. His wife tells him about the letter from Joanne.

Mrs. Yates: Hello, dear.

Mr. Yates: How are you?

Mrs. Yates: Great! Look, we have a letter from Joanne.

Mr. Yates: What _does_ she say? Please read it to me.

Mrs. Yates: She say _s_____ she's in her new place.

Mr. Yates: _Does___ she live in a house or in an apartment?

Mrs. Yates: She live _____ in an apartment.

Mr. Yates: _____ she live far from work?

Mrs. Yates: No, she _____.

Mr. Yates: How _____ she get to work?

Mrs. Yates: She say _____ she walk _____ to work and school.

Mr. Yates: To school? _____ she go to school, too?

Mrs. Yates: Yes, she _____.

Mr. Yates: Good for her!

Mrs. Yates: Dear?

Mr. Yates: Yes, what is it?

Mrs. Yates: I want to read you the letter. Please _____ interrupt!

Mr. Yates: Yes, dear.

does	don't
s	doesn't

GRAMMAR   Verb + Infinitive

- *We often use an infinitive after verbs.*

EXAMPLES   *Infinitive*

I	**need**	**to go**	to work.
Mona	**wants**	**to register**	for a typing class.
Joanne	**likes**	**to work.**	

PAIR PRACTICE   *Talk with another student. Use the phrases below.*

Student 1: What do you like/need to do ....?
Student 2: I like/need to ....
          What about you?
Student 1: I like/need to ....

1. in the morning
2. in the afternoon
3. in the evening
4. at night
5. on Saturday morning

6. on Saturday afternoon
7. on Saturday evening
8. on Sunday
9. every day
10. ....

WHAT DO YOU LIKE TO DO IN THE MORNING?

I LIKE TO READ THE NEWSPAPER. WHAT ABOUT YOU?

PAIR PRACTICE   *Talk with another student. Answer in your own words.*

Student 1: What do you want to do ....?
Student 2: I want to ....

1. at the break
2. before school
3. after class
4. on Sunday
5. on Saturday

6. on Friday evening
7. now
8. tomorrow
9. in June
10. ....

WHAT DO YOU WANT TO DO AT THE BREAK?

I WANT TO REST.

WRITE   *Fill in the blanks with* **like, want,** *or* **need** *and an infinitive.*

WHAT DO YOU WANT TO DO THIS WEEKEND?

MAYBE.

On Saturday, I _____ ___ _____ in the morning. Then I

_____ ___ _____ in the afternoon. Don't forget, you _____

_____ ___ _____. Do you ____ _____ ___ _____ in the evening?

READ

Roberto and Raymond get a letter from Italy.

> Dear Roberto and Raymond,
>
> Look! This is my first letter in English. Now I can practice my English in my letters to you. The family is fine and they all send you love and kisses. Life here in Italy is always the same. It never changes. I get up early, go to school, come home, play with my friends, help Mother in the kitchen, do my homework, watch some T.V., and go to bed at 9 o'clock. On Saturday, I can go to bed at 10 o'clock. You can see nothing changes.
>
> How are you? What do you do every day? How's your life there different from here? Please write and tell me.   Love,
>   Victorio
>
> P.S. Mother says to write every week.
> P.P.S. Send us a photo, too.

UNDERSTAND   *Circle Yes, he does. or No, he doesn't.*

1. Does Victorio live in this country?	Yes, he does.	No, he doesn't.
2. Does Victorio live with his parents?	Yes, he does.	No, he doesn't.
3. Does he go to bed at 10 p.m. every night?	Yes, he does.	No, he doesn't.
4. Does he study English in school?	Yes, he does.	No, he doesn't.
5. Does he want to know about life here?	Yes, he does.	No, he doesn't.

SPELLING   Third Person Singular Ending

- *For the third person singular of the present habitual tense:*

  1. add **-es** to verbs that end in **s**, **sh**, **ch**, **z**, and **x**.

  2. when words end in **y** preceded by a consonant, change the **y** to **i** and add **–es**. This is the same rule for forming plural nouns.

  3. add **–s** to most other verbs.

  EXAMPLES

  She starts work early. She punch<u>es</u> in at 8 a.m.
  She finish<u>es</u> at 5 p.m.
  She go<u>es</u> home and get<u>s</u> ready for school.
  She stud<u>ies</u> in the evening.

WRITE   *Unscramble the letters and then write the word on the line.*

Roberto: Look, a letter from Victorio!
Raymond: How is he?
Roberto: He's fine. The letter's in English.

He _Says_ he _wants_ to practice
      yass   twnas

English. He _____ English at school.
           seisutd

Raymond: What _____ he _____ about home?
         deos   yas

Roberto: He _____ nothing _____ at home.
      syas   gsecanh

He _____ up early, _____ to school,
     egts   egos

_____ mother in the kitchen, _____
  pshel   sedo

his homework, and _____ to bed at 9 p.m.
        geos

Raymond: I'm sure he _____ with his friends and
        yspal

_____ T.V., too.
  tawhcse

Roberto: I think he's right. Nothing _____ at home.
         hnacesg

LOOK, A LETTER FROM VICTORIO!

WRITE   *Write a letter to a friend or a relative about your regular activities. Use some of the words in the box below.*

go shopping	clean the house	go to bed	get up	go to work
come home	leave the house	eat	play	watch T.V.
help	visit	walk	speak to	know
get ready	work	live	buy	see
try to relax	meet a friend	have	like	want
call	study	read	do	get

Dear ⟶ _____

WRITE   *Capitalize the names and places on the envelopes.*

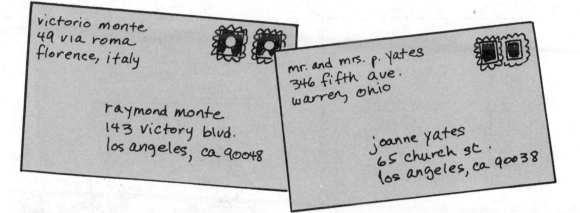

PAIR PRACTICE   *Write your name and address and your partner's name and address on the envelopes below.*

CHALLENGE   *Write a letter to a friend or relative. Address an envelope and mail it.*

READ

The mailman gives Victorio the mail.

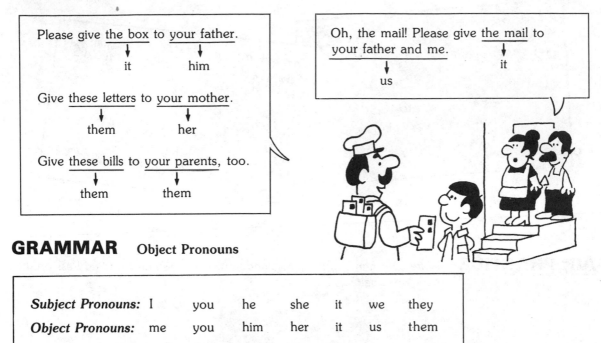

Please give the box to your father.
↓   ↓
it   him

Give these letters to your mother.
↓   ↓
them   her

Give these bills to your parents, too.
↓   ↓
them   them

Oh, the mail! Please give the mail to
your father and me.   it
↓
us

GRAMMAR   Object Pronouns

Subject Pronouns:	I	you	he	she	it	we	they
Object Pronouns:	me	you	him	her	it	us	them

● *Use object pronouns as objects in the sentence or after prepositions.*

READ   *Make complete sentences with the words in the boxes below.*

I	see		me.
You	speak with		you.
We	like		him.
They	know		her.
			it.
			us.
			them.

He	mails	it	to	me.
She	gives	them		you.
It	shows			him.
				her.
				it.
				us.
				them.

PAIR PRACTICE   *Talk with another student. Practice the phrases below.*

Student 1: Where's............?
Student 2: I don't know. Do you need
            to speak to ....?
Student 1: No, I don't. / Yes, I do.

1. your brother
2. your sister
3. your mother
4. your father
5. your family
6. your teacher
7. your friend
8. your husband/wife
9. your neighbor
10. ....

READ

Rita Landry and Raymond speak during the break.

Rita: Hi, Raymond. Can I join you?
Raymond: Sure, sit down with me.
Rita: Where's your brother?
Raymond: I don't know. Do you need to speak to him?
Rita: What's that?
Raymond: It's a letter from my parents.
We get a letter from them every week.
We have a little brother, and he writes us, too.
We get a letter from him every month or so.
Don't you get letters from your family?
Rita: Not many. I don't have a very big family.
I have only a mother and I see her every week.
How's your family?
Raymond: They're all fine.
Rita: Tell me about your family.

WRITE   *Underline all the object pronouns in the dialog above.*

WRITE   *Fill in the spaces with* **him**, **her**, *or* **them**.

My family lives in Italy.

My mother is a housewife. My

father's a small businessman.

He loves _her_ very much.

He works very hard.

My mother helps _____ on the

weekends.

Victorio is my little brother.

This letter is from _____.

What about your family? Tell _____

about _____.

I don't have a big family, but I have many

friends.

Do you know Wanda and Stephen?

They're good friends. I see _____ every

day.

And oh! Paul Green. He's in my wood shop

class. He helps _____. And Maria.

She's really nice. I come to school with

_____. And Mr. Fuller. He's wonderful. He

speaks to _____ at the break.

PAIR PRACTICE   *Fold the page in half. Look at one side only.*

Student 1	Student 2

Student 1

Listen to the questions and find the answers in this schedule.

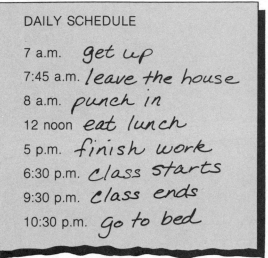

DAILY SCHEDULE

7 a.m. *get up*
7:45 a.m. *leave the house*
8 a.m. *punch in*
12 noon *eat lunch*
5 p.m. *finish work*
6:30 p.m. *class starts*
9:30 p.m. *class ends*
10:30 p.m. *go to bed*

Now, you ask these questions.

1. Are the tools next to David or Joanne?
2. Is the clock behind him or her?
3. Is the machine behind them or between them?
4. Are the lockers behind him or her?
5. Is the box in front of him or her?
6. Are the lights over or under them?

Student 2

Ask these questions.

1. When does Joanne get up?
2. When does she leave home?
3. What time does she punch in?
4. What time does school finish?
5. When does school start every day?
6. What time does Joanne leave work?
7. What time does she eat lunch?
8. When does her class begin?
9. When does she go home from class?
10. What time does she go to bed?

Now, you listen to the questions, and find the answers in the picture.

FOLD HERE

PHONICS   The Long *a* Sound (as in *mail*)

• *We sometimes write the long **a** sound as **ay** or **ai** at the end of a syllable before a consonant.*

LISTEN

Pay him.

This way please.

mail

Sunday

Wait!

LISTEN   *Circle the words that have the long **a** sound.*

1. (Sunday)   map   classroom
2. sat   Sami   yesterday
3. Raymond   father   at
4. tall   mail   lamp
5. bad   what   today
6. wait   Maria   are
7. call   Friday   Wanda
8. painter   American   wall
9. man   way   many
10. smart   day   practice

WRITE   *Write **ai** or **ay** in the spaces.*

1. Please m_*ai*_l the letters on the table tod_*ay*_.

2. S_____! Don't pl____ on the ch____r!

3. Let's do the p____r practice exercises.

4. Victorio s_____s he helps his mother every d_____.

5. Hey! R____mond! Please w____t for me!

6. Ray alw____s s____s "hello."

7

How Much Does This Cost?

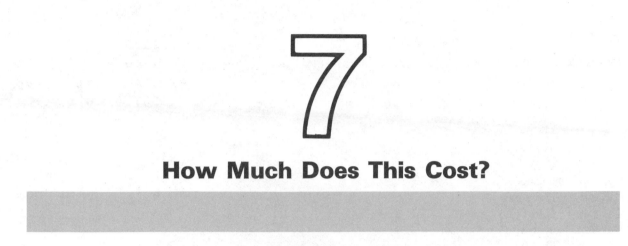

COMPETENCIES
- Counting Money
- Reading Prices
- Reading a Simple Menu
- Reading a Newspaper and Telephone Book Ads
- Getting Information About Child Care

GRAMMAR
- *how much/how many*
- *what kind of*
- *a little/a few/a lot of*

VOCABULARY
- Names of Coins
- Common Food Items
- Child Care Terms

PHONICS
- The Long *e* Sound (as in *tea*)

READ

Maria Corral and her son, José, are at a catering truck.

Customer: How much do these doughnuts cost?
Caterer: They're 35 cents each.
How many do you want?
Customer: Two doughnuts and some juice, too.
Caterer: What kind of juice?
Customer: Orange.
Caterer: Here you are.
Customer: Can you change a twenty-dollar bill?
Caterer: Just a moment. Let me check.
Oh, yes, I can. Here's your change.
Customer: Thanks a lot.

```
                    FOOD TO GO MENU

Coffee & Tea      $ .60       Soft Drinks        $ .60
Milk                .70         Cola
Juice               .50         Orange
  Apple                         Lemon
  Orange                      Potato Chips         .50
Sandwiches        $2.00       Doughnuts            .35
  Ham and Cheese              Ice Cream Cones      .55
  Tuna                          Chocolate
Apples              .35         Vanilla
Candy               .25         Strawberry
```

UNDERSTAND   *Circle **True** or **False**.*

1. One doughnut costs 40 cents.   True   False
2. Two doughnuts and some juice cost $1.20.   True   False
3. The catering truck is at the adult school.   True   False
4. The change is $18.90.   True   False
5. The caterer sells three kinds of sandwiches and one kind of juice.   True   False

READ   *Pronounce the names of the kinds of money.*

COINS			*Note:*		
a penny	=	1 cent	A twenty-dollar bill	=	a twenty (a 20)
a nickel	=	5 cents	Two five-dollar bills	=	two fives (two 5's)
a dime	=	10 cents	Three ten-dollar bills	=	three tens (three 10's)
a quarter	=	25 cents			
a half dollar	=	50 cents			
a dollar	=	100 cents			

EXAMPLE

PAIR PRACTICE   *Talk with a partner. Use the names of the coins.*

Student 1: How much is a .... and a ....?
Student 2: It's .... cents.

WRITE   *Count the money in the register and fill out the balance sheet.*

Balance Sheet

6	pennies	$.06
_____	nickels	_____
_____	dimes	_____
_____	quarters	_____
_____	half dollars	_____
	Total: $_____	

CHALLENGE   *How many coins does the caterer have?*

READ   *Pronounce the prices in the ads.*

- *Read $1.98 = one dollar and ninety-eight cents, or one ninety-eight.*
- *Read $1200. = one thousand two hundred dollars, or twelve hundred dollars.*

WANT ADS ONE LINE, ONE DAY, ONE DOLLAR	
Antique Desk	$199.99
Call Barbara	432–9106
Living room furniture, five pieces	
$1500.	463–9182
Color T.V. 2 years old	$100.
Call evenings	654–9167
Small white lamp	$12.98
Call Bill	754–1324
CAR. Blue 1972 Ford	$1250.
Weekend Sale	
Refrigerator	$189.88
Stove	$125.99
Washer and Dryer	$295.59
1249 Green St.	Open Sundays

PAIR PRACTICE   *Talk with another student about the ads above.*

Student 1: How much does the .... cost?
Student 2: It costs ....

GRAMMAR   *How much / How many*

- *Use **how much** before non-count nouns such as **water**, **food**, and **money**.*
- *Use **how many** before count nouns such as **glasses**, **cents**, **dollars**, and **cups**.*

EXAMPLES

How much	(money) does this cost?
How many	doughnuts do you want?

```
                    FOOD TO GO MENU

Coffee & Tea      $ .60      Soft Drinks          $ .60
Milk                .70      Cola
Juice               .50      Orange
  Apple                      Lemon
  Orange                     Potato Chips           .50
Sandwiches       $2.00       Doughnuts              .35
  Ham and Cheese             Ice Cream Cones        .55
  Tuna                       Chocolate
Apples              .35      Vanilla
Candy               .25      Strawberry
```

PAIR PRACTICE   *Talk with another student about the menu above.*

Student 1: How much does a .... cost?
Student 2: $ .... How many .... do you want?
Student 1: ...., please.

HOW MUCH DOES COFFEE COST?

SIXTY CENTS. HOW MANY DO YOU WANT?

ONE, PLEASE.

CHALLENGE   *How much do the following menu items cost in your town, city, school, or work? Fill in the amounts.*

```
                    FOOD TO GO MENU

Coffee & Tea      $_____    Soft Drinks        $_____
Milk              _____     Cola
Juice             _____     Orange
  Apple                       Lemon
  Orange                      Potato Chips       _____
Sandwiches        _____     Doughnuts          _____
  Ham and Cheese              Ice Cream Cones    _____
  Tuna                        Chocolate
Apples            _____     Vanilla
Candy             _____     Strawberry
```

CHALLENGE

1. How much do two sandwiches, two apples, and two cups of coffee cost?

    Calculate the amount. $_____

2. Alphabetize the menu above. Write it in your notebook.

WRITE   *Fill in the spaces with* **How much** *or* **How many**.

Customer: *How much*   do these two sandwiches cost?

  Caterer: They're two dollars each.

Customer: _____ do these apples cost?

  Caterer: Thirty–five cents each. _____ do you want?

Customer: Two. And please give me some coffee, too.

  Caterer: _____ cups?

Customer: Two. One for me and one for her.

  Caterer: Is that all?

Customer: Yes. _____ is all that?

DICTATION   *Cover the sentence under the line. Write the dictation, and then check your writing.*

Dear Theresa,

1. _____

    Please go to the store.

2. _____

    Buy some milk for breakfast.

3. _____

    Get some bread, too.

4. _____

    Here's three dollars and some change.

5. _____

    Don't drink it all tonight.

                                              Love, Mom

LISTEN

José is hungry, and he wants to eat.

Caterer:	Hi, Maria. Do you live near here?
Maria:	Yes, I do. Do you?
Caterer:	No, I don't. This is one stop on my route.
José:	Mommy, I'm hungry.
Maria:	How much does this sandwich cost?
Caterer:	Two dollars.
Maria:	Give me a sandwich, one milk, and one coffee.
Caterer:	Milk and sugar for your coffee?
Maria:	Just a little milk. Can you change a ten?
Caterer:	No, I can't. I have only a few ones and a little change left.
Maria:	I have only a ten.
Caterer:	That's OK. Pay me tonight at school.
Maria:	Thanks a lot. I appreciate it.

UNDERSTAND *Circle **True** or **False**.*

1. They all live near here.	True	False
2. Maria and the caterer are at school.	True	False
3. "One coffee" means "one cup of coffee."	True	False
4. Maria likes sugar in her coffee.	True	False
5. It's the weekend.	True	False

GRAMMAR   *a little / a few*

- Use **a little** before non-count nouns.

- Use **a few** before count nouns.

- Use **a lot of** for large numbers of both count and non-count nouns.

EXAMPLES

How much tea do you sell?	**A little**	tea.
How many apples do you sell?	**A few**	apples.
How much coffee do you sell?	**A lot of**	coffee.

PAIR PRACTICE   *Talk with another student. Use the information in the daily sales record below.*

Student 1: How much .... does a caterer sell?
                        or
                How many .... does a caterer sell?
Student 2: She sells a few / a little / a lot of ....

HOW MANY APPLES DOES A CATERER SELL?

I SELL A FEW.

DAILY SALES RECORD

	Amount (cups, cartons or cans)		Amount
Coffee	100	Soft Drinks	
Tea	10	Cola	65
Milk	25	Orange	50
Juice		Lemon	10
Apple	6	Potato Chips	30
Orange	45	Doughnuts	38
Sandwiches		Ice Cream Cones	
Ham and Cheese	45	Chocolate	25
Tuna	12	Vanilla	3
Apples	4	Strawberry	12
Candy	15		

PAIR PRACTICE   *Fold this page in half. Look at one side only.*

Student 1	Student 2

Student 1

Listen to the questions and find the answers in the typical Weekly Sales Record.

WEEKLY SALES RECORD

Mon. _____ $650.00

Tues. _____ 635.50

Wed. _____ 645.75

Thurs. _____ 520.00

Fri. _____ 310.25

Sat. _____ 235.00

TOTAL: _____

Now you ask the questions.

1. How many 20's does the caterer have?
2. How many 10's does she have?
3. Does she have many 5's?
4. Does she have money in coins?
5. Does she have a lot of 1's?
6. How much money does she have in total?

Student 2

Ask these questions.

1. How much money does the caterer make on Monday?
2. How much money does the caterer make on Saturday?
3. Does the caterer sell a lot of food on Saturday?
4. When does the caterer sell a lot of food?
5. When does the caterer sell a little food?
6. What is the total for the week?

Now you listen to the questions and find the answers on the Weekly Balance Sheet.

WEEKLY BALANCE SHEET

100 dollar bills _____ 3

50 dollar bills _____ 2

20 dollar bills _____ 80

10 dollar bills _____ 90

5 dollar bills _____ 14

1 dollar bills _____ 26

Coins _____ 2 quarters

TOTAL: _____

LISTEN

Maria asks the caterer about child care centers.

Maria: Maybe you can help me. You know a lot of people.
Caterer: What's the problem?
Maria: I want to find a child care center for my son.
Caterer: My daughter goes to the nursery school near here.
It's really nice and it's licensed.
Maria: Oh, really?
Caterer: Yeah. How old is your son?
Maria: Four years old.
Caterer: Good. They take children between 2 years 9 months and 5 years old. Go and talk to them.
Maria: What kind of facilities do they have?
Caterer: They have clean classrooms, a small gym, and a big playground.
Maria: What kind of activities do they have?
Caterer: They have time for inside and outside play, structured play, and an exercise class.
Maria: What kind of materials do they have?
Caterer: They have a lot of school materials, books, and toys.
Maria: Thanks a lot. You're a big help.
Caterer: Don't forget to take his medical records.

UNDERSTAND   *Circle True, False, or I don't know.*

1. Maria's daughter goes to nursery school.   True   False   I don't know.
2. The nursery school is near them.   True   False   I don't know.
3. Maria asks about facilities, activities, and materials.   True   False   I don't know.
4. The caterer doesn't like the nursery.   True   False   I don't know.
5. The nursery costs a lot of money.   True   False   I don't know.

CHALLENGE   *Underline **What kind of** in all the sentences in the dialog above.*

PAIR PRACTICE   *Talk with another student about the telephone book ads below.*

Student 1: What kind of .... do the schools have?

activities
facilities
materials

Student 2: ....

Happy Times Nursery School

Children pre-school and kindergarten
Ages 2 to 7
Many learning activities: swimming, dance, exercise
Summer playground (July to August)

6252 Sutter Avenue
For information call 781-5499

Play House Day Care Center

Ages: 2 1/2 to 7
Small classes
Swimming and exercise classes
Fully licensed teachers
Books and toys
Good rates

768-4270
1369 Green St.

Little Red School House

Before and after school care
Excellent playground
Summer swimming classes
12-month full- or part-time schedule
Ages 2 to 6
Hot lunches, many toys

123 Cherry Lane
Call 881-9706

CHALLENGE   *Find a nursery school ad in your local telephone book. Which do you think is the best school? Why? (Explain.)*

PHONICS   The Long *e* Sound (as in *tea*)

- We usually write the long *e* as **ee** or **ea**.

- Vowel sounds before **r** have a slightly different pronunciation.

LISTEN

eat   tea   three **3**   ice cream

street

LISTEN   *Listen to the words. Circle the words that have the long e sound.*

1. (sleep)	bed	let
2. clean	say	yes
3. see	the	pen
4. they	need	friends
5. every	desk	engineer
6. ten	speak	men
7. pencil	cents	free
8. help	seven	teachers
9. each	sell	eleven
10. coffee	twelve	caterer

WRITE   *Write ee or ea in the spaces.*

1. I **ea**t ice cr**ea**m with cl**ea**n hands.

2. I m____t and sp____k to the t____chers on the str____t ____ch day.

3. Thr____ fr____ cups of coff____ or t____ for the engin____rs, pl____se.

8

A New Student

- Review
- Test

LISTEN

Tan Tran is a new student at the adult school.

EXCUSE ME, IS THIS THE COUNSELING OFFICE?

THANK YOU.

ADULT SCHOOL OFFICE

NO, IT ISN'T. IT'S NEXT DOOR TO THE RIGHT.

Tan meets the counselor.

Counselor: May I help you?
Tan Tran: Yes, I want to register for an English class.
Counselor: What level?
Tan Tran: Level One.
Counselor: Let's fill out this registration form.

COUNSELING OFFICE →

WRITE   *Fill out the registration card for Tan Tran.*

I'M TAN TRAN. I'M FROM VIETNAM. I WANT TO STUDY ENGLISH. I WANT TO BE IN LEVEL ONE ESL. I LIVE AT 1643 SIXTH STREET IN APARTMENT FOUR, IN LOS ANGELES, CALIFORNIA. MY ZIP CODE IS 90038. MY TELEPHONE NUMBER IS SEVEN-SIX-THREE-ZERO-FOUR-TWO-ONE. MY DATE OF BIRTH IS JUNE TWENTY-FOURTH, NINETEEN FORTY-TWO.

REGISTRATION CARD

NAME: _____
      last   first   middle

ADDRESS: _____
      number   street   apartment

CITY: _____ STATE: _____ ZIP CODE: _____

DATE OF BIRTH: _____ NATIONALITY: _____

LEVEL: _____

CLASS: _____

TELEPHONE: _____ SIGNATURE: _____

UNDERSTAND   *Circle **True** or **False**.*

1. The new student is Tan Tran.   True   False
2. His last name is Tan.   True   False
3. He's forty–two years old.   True   False
4. He doesn't have a telephone.   True   False
5. He wants to be in an ESL class.   True   False

WRITE   *Unscramble the letters and then write them on the lines.*

The counselor gives Tan his registration card.

HERE'S YOUR REGISTRATION CARD.

Secretary: *Here's* your identification card.
reHe's

Tan Tran: Thank you.

Secretary: Now *give* this registration card to your teacher in Room 124.
vige

Tran enters the classroom.

I'M A NEW STUDENT.

Tan Tran: I'm a new student.

Mr. Barns: Please _____ in. _____ your registration card.
emoc   eherWs'

Tan Tran: Is this what you _____?
twan

Mr. Barns: Yes, _____ it. Oh, the bell! _____ take a break.
atth's   etL's

Tan meets the ESL students.

Maria: Hi. I'm Maria Corral.

Tan Tran: _____ to meet you.
ePaedls

Maria: Me, too. _____ are you from?
erWeh

Tan Tran: Vietnam.

Maria: Are you _____?
rrmidea

Tan Tran: Yes, I am. I _____ a wife and two sons.
veha

Maria: _____ do you do?
taWh

Tan Tran: I'm a welder. I _____ in the lamp factory on 5th St.
korw

Maria: You're lucky. I _____ have a job.
tod'n

Tan Tran: _____ and _____ the personnel manager at the factory.
oG   ese

Maybe he can _____ you a job.
igve

Maria: Thanks a lot.

READ

Maria asks for directions.

Now Maria asks for an application.

Maria: Is this the personnel office?
Receptionist: No, it's upstairs. Here's an application. Fill it out first.
Maria: What room is the personnel office in?
Receptionist: It's upstairs to the left in Room 213.

DIRECTORY	
President	101
Vice President	102
Personnel Manager	213
Secretary	103
Receptionist	104
Accountant	214
Receiving Dept.	110
Shipping Dept.	111
Maintenance Dept.	112
Work Supervisor	315

PAIR PRACTICE   *Talk with another student about the directory above.*

Student 1: What room is the .... in?
Student 2: In Room ....
Student 2: What floor is the .... on?
Student 1: On the .... floor.

WHAT ROOM IS THE ACCOUNTANT IN?

WHAT FLOOR IS THE PRESIDENT ON?

IN ROOM TWO-ONE-FOUR.

ON THE FIRST FLOOR.

PAIR PRACTICE   *Talk with another student about the directory above.*

Student 1: Who's/What's in Room ....?
Student 2: .... is.

WHAT'S IN ROOM ONE-TEN?

THE RECEIVING DEPARTMENT IS.

WRITE   *Fill out the application form for Maria. Use the information on the identification card.*

IDENTIFICATION CARD

Name: *Maria Corral*

Address: *396 Ship St.*

Santa Monica, CA 92069

Telephone: *787- 6935*

Occupation: *Cashier*

Date of birth: *4* / *3* / *1961*

Class: *ESL*   Level: *One*

APPLICATION FOR EMPLOYMENT _____ Today's Date: _____

NAME: _____ _____ _____
         last   first   middle

ADDRESS: _____ apartment
          number   street

CITY: _____ STATE: _____ TELEPHONE: _____

                          NATIONALITY: _____

OCCUPATION: _____

WRITE   *Now you fill out an application for the job, too.*

APPLICATION FOR EMPLOYMENT

NAME: _____ Today's Date: _____
        last   first   middle

ADDRESS: _____
          number   street   apartment

CITY: _____ STATE: _____ TELEPHONE: _____

OCCUPATION: _____ NATIONALITY: _____

When can you begin to work? _____

Can you work on weekends? _____

Can you work at night? _____

Your last job: Where? _____ When? _____

Do you have a job now? _____

                    SIGNATURE: _____

READ

Maria is in the personnel office.

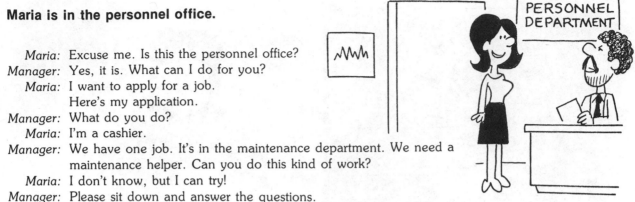

Maria:	Excuse me. Is this the personnel office?
Manager:	Yes, it is. What can I do for you?
Maria:	I want to apply for a job. Here's my application.
Manager:	What do you do?
Maria:	I'm a cashier.
Manager:	We have one job. It's in the maintenance department. We need a maintenance helper. Can you do this kind of work?
Maria:	I don't know, but I can try!
Manager:	Please sit down and answer the questions.

QUESTIONNAIRE

Put a check (✓) under YES or NO.

	Yes	No	Yes	No
1. Can you work on the weekends?	✓			
2. Can you work at night?	✓			
3. Do you have a job now?		✓		
4. Can you begin now?	✓			
5. Can you fix machines and equipment?		✓		
6. Do you learn quickly?	✓			
7. Do you work well with people?	✓			
8. Can you read and write in English?	✓			
9. Are you a careful worker?	✓			
10. Can you use simple tools?	✓			

WRITE   *You fill in the second questionnaire above.*

PAIR PRACTICE   *Ask and answer the questions in the questionnaire above with another student.*

LISTEN

Maria gets the job.

Manager: Can you do maintenance work?

Maria: What kind of work is it?

Manager: A maintenance helper checks and cleans the factory equipment, replaces parts, and uses simple tools and materials.

Maria: I see.

Manager: Can you do all that?

Maria: I can try. I'm a good worker and I learn quickly.

Manager: OK. You can begin a short training period on Monday.

Maria: Thanks a lot.

Manager: Here's the work schedule for Monday.

Work Schedule	Date: *Monday*
8 a.m.	*punch in, meet supervisor*
9 a.m.	*begin training*
10 a.m.	*fill out forms*
11 a.m.	*help fix the clock in the workshop*
12 noon	*have lunch*
1 p.m.	*replace lightbulbs in halls*
2 p.m.	*help fix broken tables in lunchroom*
3 p.m.	*check machine in the office*
4 p.m.	*clean up*
5 p.m.	*punch out*

UNDERSTAND   *Circle True, False, or I don't know.*

1. Can Maria do maintenance work?   True   False   I don't know.
2. A training period is a learning period.   True   False   I don't know.
3. Maria works eight hours a day.   True   False   I don't know.

WRITE   *Now, you write your daily schedule for Monday.*

Work Schedule   Date: _____

8 a.m. _____   1 p.m. _____

9 a.m. _____   2 p.m. _____

10 a.m. _____   3 p.m. _____

11 a.m. _____   4 p.m. _____

12 noon   5 p.m. _____

PAIR PRACTICE   *Talk with another student about the schedule above.*

Student 1: What do you do at ....?
Student 2: I .... What about you?
Student 1: I ....

WHAT DO YOU DO AT 12 NOON?
I HAVE LUNCH. WHAT ABOUT YOU?
I HAVE LUNCH, TOO.

DICTATION   *Cover the sentences below the line. Write the dication, and then check your writing.*

Dear Mario,

1. _____
I have a new job!

2. _____
It's on Fifth Street near the nursery school.

3. _____
I begin on Monday morning at 8 a.m.

4. _____
Please don't eat when you get home.

5. _____
Let's all go to a restaurant tonight, OK?

6. _____
I'm at the nursery school now.

7. _____
Be back at 4:30 or 5 o'clock.

8. _____
See you then.

Love, Maria

TEST   *Circle the correct answer.*

1. How much _____ they?
   a. is   c. am
   b. are   d. cost

2. Pleased to meet you. Pleased to meet you, _____.
   a. to   c. too
   b. two   d. tu

3. I'm a new student. _____ my registration card.
   a. This   c. Here's
   b. These   d. Those

4. Mario's _____ electrician.
   a. a   c. and
   b. an   d. am

5. Five plus three _____ eight.
   a. equals   c. minus
   b. do   d. plus

6. Thank you. _____ welcome.
   a. You   c. Your
   b. You'r   d. You're

7. Please stand up and go _____ the chalkboard.
   a. up   c. at
   b. to   d. in

8. Come on. _____ go to the snack bar.
   a. Let   c. Let's
   b. We   d. Us

9. Please pick _____ the box.
   a. up   c. on
   b. down   d. in

10. These shoes are old and torn. I need _____ new shoes.
    a. a little   c. some
    b. much   d. a lot

11. The shoe sale is _____ the first and second day of the month.
    a. in   c. on
    b. at   d. to

12. What floor is the store _____?
    a. in   c. on
    b. at   d. to

13. What room is the office in? It's on the _____ floor.
    a. two   c. three
    b. second   d. one

14. Can you tell me _____ the office is?
    a. when   c. where
    b. who   d. what time

15. Please _____ in this application.
    a. write   c. read
    b. fill   d. full

16. Please get me the box _____ the machine.
    a. between   c. next
    b. front   d. next to

17. Please spell your _____ name.
    a. one   c. big
    b. last   d. small

18. Let's talk about it _____.
    a. before   c. yesterday
    b. next   d. tomorrow

19. Please _____ forget to water the plants.
    a. do   c. don't
    b. doesn't   d. does

20. What do you do _____ morning.
    a. in   c. in the
    b. at the   d. on the

21. Let's have a party _____ Saturday evening.
    a. at   c. to
    b. on   d. in

22. I take a vacation _____ June.
    a. in   c. to
    b. on   d. at

23. Los Angeles and New York are big
    _____.
    a. cities   c. citys
    b. city   d. cityes

24. Joanne Yates _____ to school.
    a. goes   c. gos
    b. goez   d. goss

25. Please _____ interrupt me when I
    speak!
    a. doesn't   c. doen't
    b. don't   d. does

26. Joanne _____ go to school on
    Sunday.
    a. isn't   c. doesn't
    b. aren't   d. don't

27. Victorio is my little brother. This letter is
    from _____.
    a. he   c. her
    b. him   d. them

28. My parents live in Italy. I love _____
    very much.
    a. them   c. him
    b. they   d. her

29. _____ does this cost?
    a. How many   c. What kind of
    b. How much   d. What kind

30. How many doughnuts _____?
    a. want you   c. does you want
    b. do you   d. you want
       want

31. How much money _____ the caterer
    have?
    a. are   c. does
    b. do   d. is

32. _____ ice cream do you want?
    a. How many   c. How
    b. What kind   d. What kind of

33. Can you change a ten dollar _____ ?
    a. bill   c. money
    b. coin   d. paper

34. The caterer sells _____ coffee.
    a. a few   c. a lot
    b. few   d. a lot of

35. What kind of activities does the nursery
    school _____?
    a. take   c. are
    b. give   d. have

36. How old _____ your son?
    a. are   c. is
    b. have   d. be

37. David and Sami are _____.
    a. man   c. mans
    b. men   d. mens

38. Joanne and Rita are _____.
    a. woman   c. wemen
    b. womans   d. women

39. Mr. and Mrs. Barns have two _____.
    a. children   c. childrens
    b. childs   d. child

40. Who are those _____ over there?
    a. peoples   c. womens
    b. people   d. mens

Let's Have a Garage Sale

COMPETENCIES	• Describing and Telling Location of Objects
GRAMMAR	• *there is/there are*
	• *some/any*
	• Adjective Word Order
VOCABULARY	• Common Household Items
	• Descriptive Adjectives
	• Names of Community Areas and Buildings
	• *both*
PHONICS	• The Long *u* Sound (as in *room*)

LISTEN

James Fuller and his wife, Betty, are in the garage.

> **Betty:** Today's Saturday.
> Come on, let's clean out the garage.
> **James:** There's a lot of junk here.
> **Betty:** There sure is!
> **James:** Look! There's my old bicycle over there in the corner.
> **Betty:** And there are my old flower pots under the workbench.
> **James:** Yeah, and they're all broken, too.
> There are pieces all over the floor.
> **Betty:** Let's put them in the trash.
> **James:** Get a garbage can.
> There's one behind the house.
> **Betty:** Only one? One isn't big enough for all this junk.

UNDERSTAND   *Circle True, False, or We don't know.*

1. It's the weekend.	True	False	We don't know.
2. The junk isn't in the house.	True	False	We don't know.
3. Betty can use the flower pots.	True	False	We don't know.
4. The bicycle is broken.	True	False	We don't know.
5. "Trash" means "garbage."	True	False	We don't know.

WRITE   *Underline **there's** and **there are** in all the sentences in the dialog above.*

GRAMMAR   *there is / there are*

- **There's (there is)** *is for a singular noun.*
- **There are** *is for a plural noun.*

EXAMPLES

		Place
There's	a bicycle	**in the corner.**
There isn't	room	**in the garbage can.**
There are	flower pots	**under the workbench.**

READ   *Make complete sentences with the words in the box below.*

There's	a lot of junk	in the garage.
There isn't	room	on the workbench.
There are	flower pots	under the workbench.
There aren't	tools	in the garbage can.
		on the floor.

GRAMMAR   Questions and Short Answers

EXAMPLES

Questions	*Short Answers*
Is there a bicycle in the corner?	**Yes, there is.**
Is there a bicycle under the workbench?	**No, there isn't.**
Are there flower pots under the workbench?	**Yes, there are.**
Are there flower pots in the corner?	**No, there aren't.**

PAIR PRACTICE   *Ask and answer questions about the picture on the previous page. Use the short answers.*

Student 1: Is there a .... in the garage?
Student 2: Yes, there is. / No, there isn't.
Student 1: Are there .... in the garage?
Student 2: Yes, there are. / No, there aren't.

IS THERE A BICYCLE IN THE GARAGE?

YES, THERE IS.

LISTEN

Betty and James decide to have a garage sale.

James: What can we do with all this junk?
      Do you have any ideas?
 Betty: Let's have a garage sale.
James: A garage sale?
 Betty: Why throw all this junk away?
      Let's sell it and make some money.
James: That sounds good to me.
      Let's move all this stuff to the driveway.

Customer: Are there any old books here for sale?
   James: No, there aren't any.
Customer: Are there any old records?
   James: Yes, there are some in the pile next to the bicycle.
Customer: How much are they?
   James: Fifty cents each.
Customer: Sold!
   James: Great, our first customer!

UNDERSTAND   *Circle* **True**, **False**, *or* **We don't know.**

1. "That sounds good" means "That's a good idea."   True   False   We don't know.
2. "All this stuff" means "all these things."   True   False   We don't know.
3. The old books are in a pile.   True   False   We don't know.
4. There are a lot of old records.   True   False   We don't know.
5. The customer wants the old records.   True   False   We don't know.

GRAMMAR   *some / any*

* We generally use **any** in questions and with negatives, and **some** in the affirmative.

EXAMPLES

Are there	**any**	old books?	No, there aren't **any.**
Are there	**any**	old records?	Yes, there are **some** in a pile.

PAIR PRACTICE   *Talk with another student about the picture below.*

Student 1: Are there any .... in the driveway?
Student 2: Yes, there are some. / No, there aren't any.

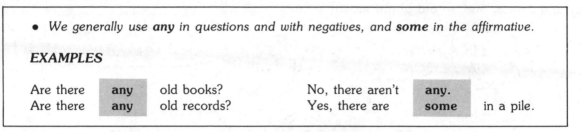

PAIR PRACTICE   *Talk with another student about the picture above.*

Student 1: How many .... are there?
Student 2: There's only one.
             or
There are ....
             or
There aren't any.

LISTEN

Betty and James find an old photo album.

PAIR PRACTICE

Talk with another student about the picture below.

Student 1: There's a ....
Student 2: And there are ...., too.

PAIR PRACTICE

Talk with another student. Describe where things are in the picture above.

Student 1: Look! There's a .... next to the.................
Student 2: And there are .... near the ...., too.

LISTEN

James finds a picture of his hometown, too.

James: And look at this photo. Here's Campbell, my hometown.
Betty: There's a big difference between our hometowns.
James: No, there isn't.
Betty: Yes, there is. There's a beautiful park in Warren, but not in Campbell.
James: Well, there's a nice church in both pictures.
Betty: There are some theaters in Warren, but not in Campbell.

UNDERSTAND   *Circle **True** or **False**.*

1. Both photos are the same.   True   False
2. There's a park in only one photo.   True   False
3. There's a church in only one photo.   True   False

PAIR PRACTICE   *Find the differences and similarities in the two pictures below.*

Student 1: There's/There are .... in Warren, but not in Campbell.
Student 2: There's/There are .... in both towns.

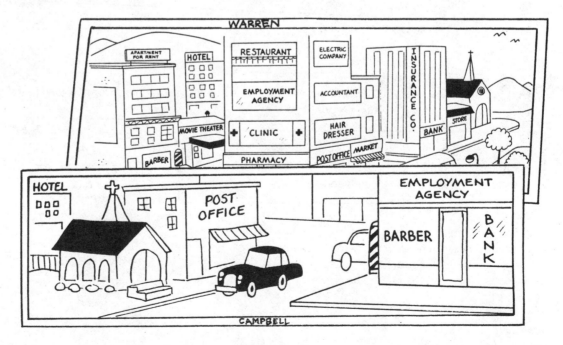

DRAW   *Draw a map or picture of your hometown. You can include some of these places.*

home	store	bank	airport	bus stop	factory
hospital	park	church	post office	market	office
restaurant	museum	river	lake	mountains	hills
beach	school	zoo	library	university	theater

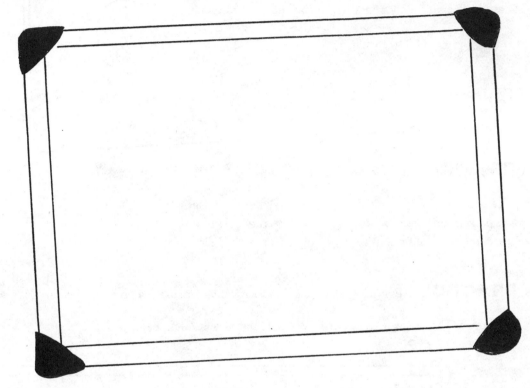

PAIR PRACTICE   *Ask and answer questions about places in your hometown. Use the following prepositions:*

in	in front of	next to	to the left of
on	behind	near	to the right of
over	under	between	across from

Student 1: Is there a .... in your hometown?
Student 2: Yes, there is. It's .... the ....
             or
             No, there isn't.

IS THERE A FACTORY IN YOUR HOMETOWN?

YES, THERE IS. IT'S BEHIND THE MOVIE THEATER.

WRITE   *Fill in the blanks with* **there** *or* **they.**

Betty and James find more old things.

Betty: *There* are a few old lamps over the workbench.

James: Are *they* all right?

Betty: Sure, _____'re fine. Let's sell them for $5.00 each.

James: What's in that box?

Betty: _____ are some old clothes and shoes.

James: Are _____ any good clothes?

Betty: Sure, _____ are nice and clean.

James: What about the shoes?

Betty: _____ are old and torn.

James: I have an idea.

Betty: What?

James: Let's give them to the church.

Betty: That's a great idea.

James: Let's put them in a large plastic bag.

Betty: _____ aren't any bags here.

James: Where are _____?

Betty: _____ are some in the kitchen.

James: Good. Be back in a minute.

LISTEN

Betty and James find a pile of wood.

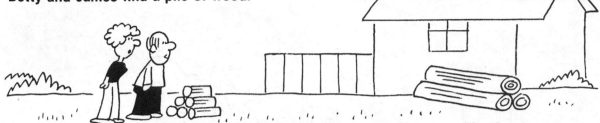

James: And what can we do with all this wood?
Betty: Let's use it for firewood this winter.
James: Put all the short, thin pieces over here in one pile.
Betty: What about all the long, thick pieces?
James: Put them over there.
Betty: I can't pick up the big, heavy pieces.
James: I can move them, and you can move the small, light pieces, OK?
Betty: That's fine with me.

WRITE   *Underline all the adjectives in the dialog above.*

GRAMMAR   Word Order

• *Notice the word order of the following adjectives. There is a comma (,) between the adjectives.*

Article	Size	Quality	Noun
the	short,	thin	pieces
the	long,	thick	pieces
the	big,	heavy	pieces
the	small,	light	pieces
a	large,	heavy	bag
a	little,	red	flower pot

READ   *Make complete sentences with the words in the box below.*

There	is isn't are aren't	a a few some any	little small big large short long	thin thick light heavy torn	(object) (thing) (objects) (things)	for sale.

PAIR PRACTICE   *Fold the page in half. Look at one side only.*

### Student 1	### Student 2

Student 1

Listen to the questions and find the answers in the picture.

Now ask these questions.

1. Is there a sale tomorrow?

2. How many different kinds of tools are there for sale?

3. Are they new or used?

4. Is there any wood for sale?

5. Are there any safety glasses for sale?

6. Are both the hammer and the saw the same price?

7. How much do the tools cost?

8. How many ads are there?

9. Are there any tool boxes?

10. How much is a workbench?

Student 2

Ask these questions.

1. Are there any children in the picture?

2. Is there a car for sale?

3. How many bicycles are there?

4. Are the bicycles on the floor?

5. How much wood is there?

6. Is there a small broken record?

7. How many pairs of shoes are there?

8. Is there a T.V. set?

9. Are there a lot of toys?

10. How many radios are there?

Now listen to the questions and find the answers in the picture.

FOLD HERE

WORD ORDER   *Write correct sentences with the words and phrases below.*

Dear Ray,

1. _____

   next door.
   There's
   garage sale
   a

2. _____

   some
   firewood
   Go and get
   the winter.
   for

3. _____

   only
   heavy
   big
   Get
   pieces.

4. _____

   any
   light
   small
   get
   pieces.
   Don't

5. _____

   a
   garage sale
   have
   Let's
   next month.

6. _____

   think
   you
   a
   Do
   it's
   good idea,
   too?

Nancy

CHALLENGE   *Make a list of things **you** can sell in a garage sale at your home.*

1. _____   3. _____   5. _____

2. _____   4. _____   6. _____

PHONICS   The Long *u* Sound (as in *room*)

> • *Write the long **u** sound as **oo**.*

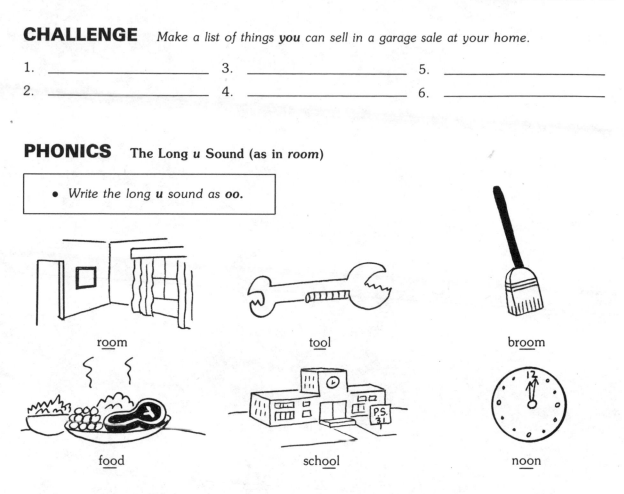

r<u>oo</u>m   t<u>oo</u>l   br<u>oo</u>m

f<u>oo</u>d   sch<u>oo</u>l   n<u>oo</u>n

LISTEN   *Listen to the words. Circle the words that have the long **u** sound.*

1. (too)   plus   not   6. goes   study   food
2. truck   classroom   one   7. tools   punch   does
3. picture   number   school   8. home   about   broom
4. soda   noon   problem   9. Saturday   Monday   restroom
5. some   afternoon   locker   10. adult   room   August

WRITE   *Unscramble the letters under the lines.*

1. Please put the *tools* and the *broom* in the closet.
               sloto   ombro

2. I choose _____ in a cafeteria at twelve _____ .
           ofdo   onno

3. Do you go to _____ in the _____ , _____ ?
           colsoh   ofrnaoten   oto

10

Do You Have an Apartment for Rent?

COMPETENCIES	• Renting an Apartment
	• Filling out an Application Form
	• Reading Apartment Ads
GRAMMAR	• *have/has*
VOCABULARY	• Rooms of the House
	• Household Appliances and Amenities
	• Common Abbreviations Used in Apartment Ads
PHONICS	• The *k* Sound

LISTEN

Mona Boulos calls Ann Porter about an apartment for rent.

Mona: Hello, my name's Mona Boulos. Do you have a house for rent?
Ann: No, I don't, but I have an unfurnished apartment for rent.
Mona: How many rooms does it have?
Ann: It has two large bedrooms, one bathroom, a living room, and a kitchen.
Mona: Does it have a den?
Ann: No, it doesn't have a den, but it has new carpets and draperies.
Mona: Does it have any kitchen appliances?
Ann: Yes, it does. It has a stove and refrigerator.
Mona: How much is the rent?
Ann: Four hundred dollars a month.
Mona: Can I make an appointment to see it?
Ann: Sure. Do you have any free time this afternoon?
Mona: Yes, I do. Is two o'clock convenient for you?
Ann: That's fine. The address is 1243 Maple Street. See you at two.

UNDERSTAND   *Circle **True**, **False**, or **We don't know**.*

1. There isn't any furniture in the apartment.   True   False   We don't know.
2. The kitchen appliances are new.   True   False   We don't know.
3. The apartment has six rooms.   True   False   We don't know.
4. Ann can show the apartment at 2 o'clock.   True   False   We don't know.
5. "A convenient time" means "a good time."   True   False   We don't know.

WRITE   *Underline **have** and **has** in the sentences in the dialog above.*

GRAMMAR   The Verb *to have*

- *The verb **to have** has an irregular form in the third person affirmative singular of the present tense: **has.***

EXAMPLES

Question Form

Do	you	**have**	a house for rent?
Do	you	**have**	any free time this afternoon?
Does	it	**have**	draperies?
Does	it	**have**	any kitchen appliances?
How many rooms	**does**	it	**have**	?

Affirmative

I	**have**	an apartment for rent.
It	**has**	two large bedrooms.

Negative

I	**don't have**	a house for rent.
It	**doesn't have**	a den.

Short Answers

Do you have a house for rent?	**Yes, I do.**	or	**No, I don't.**
Does it have draperies?	**Yes, it does.**	or	**No, it doesn't.**
Does she have any free time?	**Yes, she does.**	or	**No, she doesn't.**

READ   *Make complete sentences with the words in the box below.*

Mona Boulos		some free time today.
Ann Porter	have	an unfurnished apartment for rent.
Mr. and Mrs. Porter		new draperies and carpets.
The apartment	has	an appointment at 2 o'clock.
Ann and Mona		two bedrooms.
I		

READ

Before their appointment, Mona Boulos and Ann Porter are making lists of items.

Ask Mrs. Porter: Does the apartment have...
1. a dishwasher,
2. a balcony,
3. appliances,
4. a big yard,
5. a basement,
6. a laundry room,
7. a pool,
8. a garage,
9. an air conditioner,
10. security locks?

Tell Mrs. Boulos: The apartment has...
1. new draperies and carpets
2. a refrigerator and stove,
3. a two-car garage,
4. a backyard,
5. an air conditioner,
6. a new heater,
7. a laundry room,
8. strong locks,
9. a fireplace,
10. a smoke detector.

PAIR PRACTICE   *Tell about the apartment. What does it have? What doesn't it have?*

Student 1: The apartment has ....
Student 2: It doesn't have ....

THE APARTMENT HAS NEW DRAPES AND CARPETS.

IT DOESN'T HAVE A DISHWASHER.

CHALLENGE   *Make a list of items that your apartment has and doesn't have.*

My apartment has ....

1. _____
2. _____
3. _____
4. _____
5. _____
6. _____
7. _____

My apartment doesn't have ....

1. _____
2. _____
3. _____
4. _____
5. _____
6. _____
7. _____

READ   *Read the newspaper ads. Then cover the ads on the right. Read aloud the ads on the left.*

CONDO* 3 bd/2ba nu cpt/drps pool, sec. bldg open daily 8–5 653–9410	CONDOMINIUM three bedrooms and two bathrooms new carpets and drapes swimming pool, security building open daily from 8 a.m. to 5 p.m. 653–9410
UNF. HSE 2 bdrm frig & stv lg. bckyd wshr/dryr call aft 463–9213	UNFURNISHED HOUSE two bedrooms refrigerator and stove large backyard washer and dryer call in the afternoon 463–9213
UNF. APT 2 + 2 2–car gar. w/fplc, D–wash call for appt. 694–3012	UNFURNISHED APARTMENT two bedrooms and two bathrooms two–car garage with a fireplace, dishwasher call for an appointment 694–3012
UNFURN APT 1 bdr + den C/D, balc. no pets, $300. mo call aft 6 pm 643–9987	UNFURNISHED APARTMENT one bedroom and a den carpets and drapes, balcony no pets, $300. rent a month call after 6 p.m. 643–9987
FURN SING elev., pkg., A/C appl. xlnt oond $75. wk. call mgr. eve. 663–5401	FURNISHED SINGLE APARTMENT elevator, parking, air conditioning appliances, excellent condition $75. rent a week call the manager in the evenings 663–5401

PAIR PRACTICE   *Talk with another student about the ads above.*

Student 1: Does the .... have ....?
Student 2: Yes, it does. / No, it doesn't.

CHALLENGE   *Write the full words for the abbreviations to the left.*

UNF. APT. *Unfurnished apartment* _____

1 Bdrm D/C _____

lg. bckyd _____

A/C, frig/stv. _____

$200.mo 694–3210 _____

---

* See page 175 for more abbreviations.

WRITE   *Fill in the blanks with* **have** *or* **has.**

Mona Boulos and her husband, Peter, read the newspaper.

Peter: Does the newspaper _____ any good apartment ads?

Mona: Yes, it _____ a few.

Peter: Do any of them _____ low rent?

Mona: Most of them _____ high rents, but one _____ a very low rent. And it
_____ an air conditioner, too.

Peter: Does it _____ a yard?

Mona: Maybe it _____ a yard because it _____ a pool.

Peter: Why don't you call and ask about it?

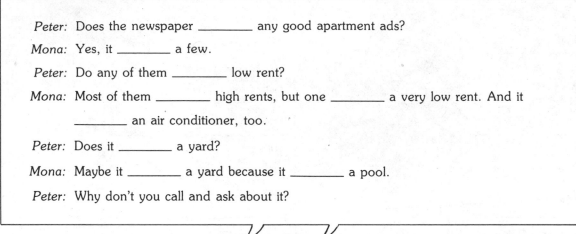

WRITE   *Fill in the missing parts of the dialog with complete sentences.*

Mona calls about the ad.

Mona: _____?
Woman: Yes, I have an apartment for rent.

Mona: _____?
Woman: It has one bedroom, a bathroom, a living room, and a small kitchen.

Mona: _____?
Woman: Yes, it has drapes and carpets, but it doesn't have a refrigerator or a stove.

Mona: _____?
Woman: It's four hundred dollars a month.

Mona: _____.
Woman: That's OK. There's no problem. Good luck. Good-bye.

LISTEN

Peter and Mona Boulos meet Paul Green at the apartment.

Mona: Hello, we have an appointment with Mrs. Porter.
Paul: Oh, yes, she's on her way. Please wait here.
I'm Paul Green. I'm the apartment building manager.
Is the appointment about the vacant apartment?
Mona: Yes, it is.
Paul: Here's an application form. You can fill it out now.
New tenants must pay the first and last months' rent and a $150 security deposit.
Mona: Thank you, we understand.

APPLICATION

NAME: *Peter and Mona Boulos*   Date: *Nov. 6*

ADDRESS: *23 Shell Ave. #6*
Los Angeles, California   TELEPHONE: *643-9821*

How long at the above address? —— years *6* months
Apartment owner's name: *Mrs. Clara Gati* Telephone: *763-1226*
Apartment owner's address: *369 Studio St. Santa Monica*
Where do you work? *Art Store* How long? —— years *4* months
Address: *4187 Simpson Ave., Studio City 91607*
Supervisor's name: *Isabel Sosa*   Work telephone: *694-1298*
How many people occupy your apartment? *2 people*
How many children do you have? *none*
How many pets do you have? *one* What kind of pets? *cat*

Please list two references below:
1. Name: *Roy Ahuna* Address: *63 Shell Ave.* Telephone: *694-9876*
2. Name: *John Craig* Address: *116 Fulton Ave.* Telephone: *946-6798*

Signature: *Peter Boulos*
Mona Boulos

WRITE   *Put the sentences of the dialog in the correct order. Write the numbers 1 to 8 in front of the sentences.*

Ann Porter shows Mona and Peter the apartment.

_____ Here it is. It needs a good cleaning.

_____ Yes, I am. Are you Mr. and Mrs. Boulos?

_____ On December 1st. Is that all right?

_____ Pleased to meet you. Let me show you the apartment.

_____ Yes, we are.

_____ Hello, are you Mrs. Porter?

_____ Yes, that's fine.

_____ That's OK. When can we move in?

WRITE   *You fill out an application for the apartment, too.*

APPLICATION

NAME: _____ Date: _____

ADDRESS: _____

_____ TELEPHONE: _____

How long at the above address? _____ years _____ months

Apartment owner's name: _____ Telephone: _____

Apartment owner's address: _____

Where do you work? _____ How long? _____ years _____ months

Address: _____

Supervisor's name: _____ Work telephone: _____

How many people occupy your apartment? _____

How many children do you have? _____

How many pets do you have? _____ What kind of pets? _____

Please list two references below:

1. Name: _____ Address: _____ Telephone: _____

2. Name: _____ Address: _____ Telephone: _____

Signature: _____

PAIR PRACTICE   *Fold the page in half. Look at one side only.*

Student 1	Student 2

Student 1

Listen to the questions and find the answers in the ads below.

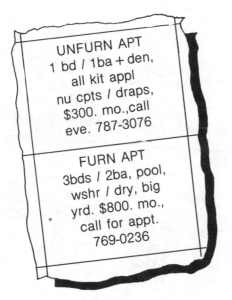

UNFURN APT
1 bd / 1ba + den,
all kit appl
nu cpts / draps,
$300. mo.,call
eve. 787-3076

FURN APT
3bds / 2ba, pool,
wshr / dry, big
yrd. $800. mo.,
call for appt.
769-0236

Now ask these questions.

1. Are there any houses for rent?
2. How many bathrooms do the apartments have?
3. How much is the rent?
4. Do both apartments have garages?
5. When can I call about the apartments?
6. What kind of appliances do the apartments have?
7. How many people can live in the unfurnished apartment?
8. Are the apartments safe?
9. Which apartment costs more? Why?

Student 2

Ask these questions.

1. How many ads are there?
2. What kind of ads are they?
3. How many rooms does each apartment have?
4. Is there a stove in any apartment?
5. Do both apartments have draperies?
6. When can I call about the apartments?
7. Do both apartments have furniture?
8. How many bathrooms does the furnished apartment have?
9. How many bedrooms does the unfurnished apartment have?
10. Which apartment costs more? Why?

Now listen to the questions and find the answers in the ads below.

FURN APT
2b + 2b cpts&drps
frig / stv / D-wash
2-car gar.$500.mo
call between 8-5
997-6543

UNFURN APT
single + pkg
sec. bldg. balc.
xlnt cond. $300 mo
call aft 5pm
996-4433

FOLD HERE

PHONICS   The *k* Sound

- The **k** sound is often spelled with the letter **k**.

- It is also spelled with the letter **c** before **a, o, u, r,** and **l.**

EXAMPLES

| drink | kitchen | week | book | walk |
| cat | cup | coin | ice cream | class |

LISTEN   *Listen to the words. Circle the words that have the **k** sound.*

1. (can)   cent   machine
2. each   correct   city
3. place   teacher   key
4. piece   price   chocolate
5. cake   center   exercise

6. company   juice   sentence
7. office   receive   coffee
8. maintenance   space   record
9. child   know   take
10. ask   watch   much

WRITE   *Write the letters **c** or **k** in the spaces below.*

1. I li _k_ e to drin _k_ ____ups of ____offee and cho____olate mil____.

2. The ____at wal____s a____ross the street ____arefully.

3. ____an you ____ome here from the ____itchen and loo____ at this bro____en re____ord?

4. This ____arton of ice ____ream ____osts $1.65.

COMMON ABBREVIATIONS USED IN APARTMENT ADS

A

advertisement	ad.
after	aft.
afternoon	aft.
air conditioner	air; a/c; AC
and	&; /
apartment	apt.
appliance	appl
appointment	appt.

B

bachelor apartment	bach.
backyard	bckyd.
balcony	balc.
bathroom	ba.; bath.
beautiful	beaut.
bedroom	bd.; bdr.; br.; bdrm.
building	bldg.
built-in cabinets	bltins

C

carpets	cpts.
carpet and drapes	cpt/drps; c/d
condominium	condo

D

decorated	dec.
deposit	dep.
dining room	din.rm.
dishwasher	D-wash; dshwshr.
drapes, draperies	drps.
dryer	dry.; dryr.

E

elevator	elev.
excellent	xlnt.

F

family room	fam. rm.
fireplace	frplc.; fplc.
first and last months' rent	1st/last
floors	flrs.
freeway	fwy.
furnished	furn.

G

garage	gar.
garden	gard.
good	gd.
good location	gd. loc.

H

hardwood floors	hdwd. flrs.
hour	hr.
house	hse.

J

jacuzzi	jac.

K

kitchen	kit.

L

large	lg.;lge.
lease	lse.
location	loc.
luxury	lux.

M

male or female	m/f
manager	mgr.
month	mo.

N

near	nr.
new	nu.

O

owner	own.
or	/

P

paid	pd.
parking	pkg.
plus	+
private party	p/p; prvtprty

R

references required	refs. req.
refrigerator	refrig.; frig.
room	rm.

S

security	sec.
security deposit	sec. dep.
separate	sep.
single apartment	sing.
subterranean (underground) parking	subt. pkg.

T

townhouse	twnhse.

U

unfurnished	unf.; unfurn.
utilities	utils.
utilities paid	utils. pd.

V

view	vu.

W

washer	wash.; wshr.
washer and dryer	wash/dry; wshr/dryr
week	wk.
with	w/

Y

yard	yd.; yrd.
year	yr.

We Have a Tight Schedule, But We Manage

COMPETENCIES	• Telling Time
	• Taking Public Transportation
	• Reading Bus, Work, and T.V. Schedules
GRAMMAR	• *to* and *at* with Expressions of Time and Place
	• Word Order for Expressions of Place and Time
VOCABULARY	• Transportation Words
PHONICS	• Long Vowels with Final Silent *e*

LISTEN

Sami speaks to Mario at the break.

Sami: Hi, Mario. Where's Maria?
Mario: She's at the catering truck downstairs.
Sami: It's hot in here. Let's go to the window and get some air.
Mario: That's fine with me.
Sami: How's her new job?
Mario: She likes it, but she comes home a little tired.
Sami: How do you manage with a family, work, and adult school?
Mario: We have a tight schedule, but we manage OK. We all get up at six sharp. I drop off Theresa at the bus stop, and she takes the bus to school. Then, I drive downtown. Maria takes José to the nursery school at a quarter to eight, and then she walks to work. After work, I pick up my daughter at the bus stop and Maria picks up José at a quarter past five. We all meet at home about half past five. In the evening, we come to school, and the kids stay at home with a neighbor. It's true, we have a busy schedule. We save the weekends for our chores and rest.

UNDERSTAND   *Circle **True**, **False**, or **We don't know**.*

1. Mario and Sami are upstairs.	True	False	We don't know.
2. The family gets up at 6 a.m.	True	False	We don't know.
3. Mario begins work at 8 a.m.	True	False	We don't know.
4. Mario works downtown.	True	False	We don't know.
5. Mario picks up José after work.	True	False	We don't know.
6. Maria and Mario work on the weekend.	True	False	We don't know.

READ   *Telling Time.*

Study the vocabulary in the pictures below.

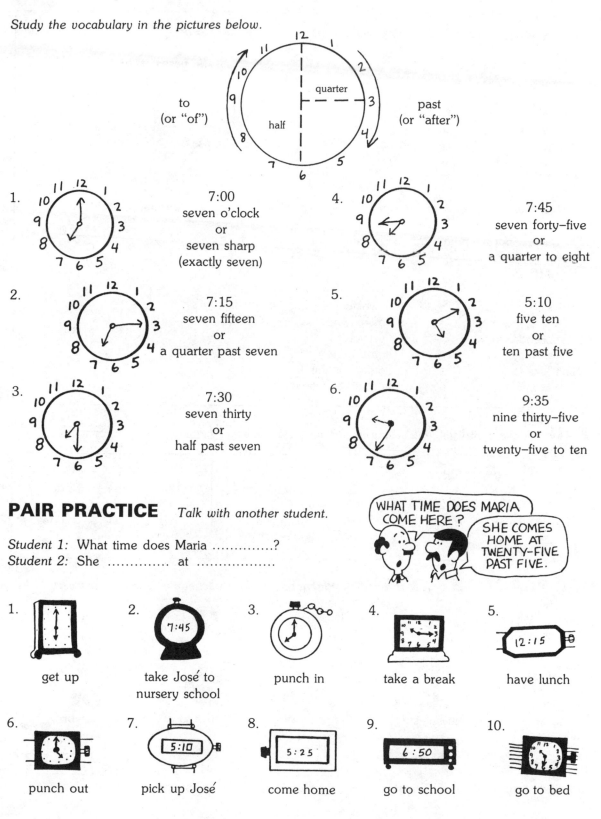

to
(or "of")

quarter

half

past
(or "after")

1. 7:00
seven o'clock
or
seven sharp
(exactly seven)

4. 7:45
seven forty–five
or
a quarter to eight

2. 7:15
seven fifteen
or
a quarter past seven

5. 5:10
five ten
or
ten past five

3. 7:30
seven thirty
or
half past seven

6. 9:35
nine thirty–five
or
twenty–five to ten

PAIR PRACTICE   *Talk with another student.*

Student 1: What time does Maria ....?
Student 2: She .... at ....

WHAT TIME DOES MARIA COME HERE?

SHE COMES HOME AT TWENTY-FIVE PAST FIVE.

1. get up

2. take José to nursery school

3. punch in

4. take a break

5. have lunch

6. punch out

7. pick up José

8. come home

9. go to school

10. go to bed

GRAMMAR   Prepositions *to* and *at*

● *Use **to** after action verbs and **at** after static verbs, especially **to be**.*

Action verbs + to			Static verbs + at		
I drive	**to**	work.	She's	**at**	the truck.
She takes the bus	**to**	school.	Let's stand	**at**	the window.
She walks	**to**	work.	I drop off Theresa	**at**	the bus stop.
We go	**to**	school.	I pick up Theresa	**at**	the bus stop.

EXCEPTIONS

● *Don't use **to** or **at** with the words **downtown**, **upstairs**, and **downstairs**.*

● *Use **at**, not **to**, before the work **home**.*

EXAMPLES

She's		downstairs.
I drive		downtown.
Mario and Sami are		upstairs.
We all meet	**at**	home.
The kids stay	**(at)**	home. (optional)
She comes		home a little tired.

READ   *Make complete sentences with the words in the boxes below.*

Do	you he she	drive work live	at	home? school? work?
Does	we they	take the bus walk	to	downtown? bus stop?

Yes,	I he she	do.
No,	we they	does.

PAIR PRACTICE   *Talk to another student about Maria's schedule. Use only the verb **to be**.*

Student 1: Where's Mario at ....?
Student 2: He's ....

PAIR PRACTICE   *Talk with another student. Use the phrases below.*

Student 1: Where are you at ....?
Student 2: I'm .... at ....
       What about you?
Student 1: I'm at .... at that time.

WHERE ARE YOU AT HALF PAST EIGHT IN THE MORNING?

I'M AT HOME AT HALF PAST EIGHT IN THE MORNING. WHAT ABOUT YOU?

I'M AT WORK AT THAT TIME.

1. half past eight in the morning
2. ten past five in the afternoon
3. quarter to eight in the evening
4. seven a.m. sharp
5. ten p.m.

6. quarter past seven in the morning
7. two to two in the afternoon
8. one to three in the afternoon
9. twenty past eleven in the morning
10. twelve sharp at night

PAIR PRACTICE   *Talk with another student about the pictures below. Use **go**, **drive**, **walk**, or other action verbs.*

Student 1: What does the Corral Family do on the weekend?
Student 2: They sometimes ....

WHAT DOES THE CORRAL FAMILY DO ON THE WEEKEND?

THEY SOMETIMES GO TO THE BEACH.

THE BEACH

the beach

NOW PLAYING

the movies

CITY PARK

the park

SHOPPING CENTER

the shopping center

CAFE

a restaurant

AL'S MARKET

the market

MUSEUM

a museum

DOWNTOWN 2 MI.

downtown

GRAMMAR   Word Order

- *We usually put expressions of place before expressions of time.*

EXAMPLES	Place	Time
1. Maria takes José	to the nursery school	in the morning.
2. I pick up my daughter	at the bus stop	after work.
3. We all meet	at home	at half past five.
4. We go	to school	in the evening.

READ   *Make complete sentences with the words and expressions in the box below. The sentences must make sense.*

Mario	is	at the nursery school	in the morning.
Maria	are	to work	at half past five.
José	drives	at home	from 8 a.m. to 5 p.m.
Theresa	walks	downtown	at a quarter to eight.
They	stays	to school	every day.
The family	takes the bus	at the bus stop	in the evening.

WRITE   *Write your daily schedule.*

	Place	Time
1. I go		
2. I walk		
3. I come		
4. I am		
5. I take the bus		
6. I stay		
7. I work		
8. I walk		
9.		
10.		

WRITE   *Fill in the spaces with **to** or **at**. If necessary, leave some lines blank.*

Mario: Well, Sami, how's your schedule?

Sami: I get up *at* a quarter *to* seven every day. I walk ____ Third Street. I wait ____ the bus stop and take the bus ____ downtown. I usually get ____ work about half past eight. I meet some friends ____ a coffee shop across the street from work and have a doughnut and coffee. I punch in ____ nine o'clock sharp. I have lunch ____ the same coffee shop ____ a quarter ____ one. I punch out ____ six, and then a friend drives me ____ home. I have a quick dinner ____ home, and then I come ____ school. It's not a bad schedule.

DICTATION   *Cover the sentences below the line. Write the dictation, and then check your writing.*

Dear Mario,

1. _____
   Please come to dinner with Wanda, Stephen, and me tonight.

2. _____
   Go to the store and buy some wine for dinner.

3. _____
   Bring Theresa with you.

4. _____
   Pick up José at the nursery school at a quarter to five.

5. _____
   Meet me at the bus stop in front of the factory at five sharp.

6. _____
   See you then.

   Love, Maria

LISTEN

Maria Corral meets Tan Tran in the lunch room at work.

Tan: Hi, Maria, how's your new job?

Maria: Fine, and thanks again for the tip about this job.

Tan: You're very welcome.
Maria, how can I get downtown by bus?
I have an appointment with the dentist this afternoon.

Maria: Take bus line 88, and then the 93.

Tan: Where can I catch them?

Maria: You can get on Bus 88 at the corner.
Get off at Third and Main Street.
Then transfer to the 93. It goes directly downtown.

Tan: How often do they run?

Maria: I have a bus schedule for the 93 in my purse.
Here it is. You can keep it.

Tan: Thanks a lot. How much is the fare?

Maria: Don't you have a monthly bus pass?

Tan: No, I don't. I don't take the bus very much.

Maria: The fare is fifty cents in exact change or a token.
Here are two tokens. Use them.

Tan: I can't take your tokens.

Maria: Please take them.

UNDERSTAND   *Circle* ***True***, ***False***, *or* ***We don't know.***

1. Tan and Maria work at the same place.	True	False	We don't know.
2. They work downtown.	True	False	We don't know.
3. Tan has a car.	True	False	We don't know.
4. Bus 88 goes directly downtown.	True	False	We don't know.
5. Two tokens cost one dollar.	True	False	We don't know.
6. "Get on" and "get off" mean the same thing.	True	False	We don't know.

PAIR PRACTICE   *Talk with another student about the bus schedule below.*

Student 1: What time does the bus stop at ....?
Student 2: It stops there at ....

> WHAT TIME DOES THE BUS STOP AT THIRD AND MAIN?

> IT STOPS THERE AT FOUR PAST THREE, TWENTY-FIVE PAST THREE, ELEVEN TO FOUR....

BUS SCHEDULE		LINE 93		
INBOUND TO DOWNTOWN				
Fifth St. & Main St.	Fourth St. & Main St.	Third St. & Main St.	Second St. & Main St.	First St. & Main St.
2:44 p.m.	2:59	3:04	3:11	3:27
3:05	3:20	3:25	3:32	3:40
3:29	3:44	3:49	3:56	4:04
4:29	4:44	4:49	4:56	5:04
5:00	5:15	5:20	5:27	5:35
5:22	5:37	5:42	5:49	5:56
5:50	6:05	6:10	6:17	6:27
6:21	6:36	6:40	6:47	6:54

PAIR PRACTICE   *Talk with another student about the bus schedule above.*

Student 1: Where does the bus stop at ....?
Student 2: It stops at the corner of .... and ....

> WHERE DOES THE BUS STOP AT FOUR PAST THREE?

> IT STOPS AT THE CORNER OF THIRD AND MAIN.

WRITE   *Fill in the blanks with the vocabulary from the box.*

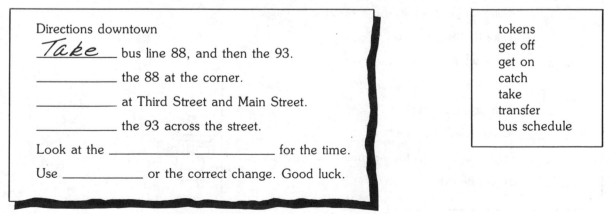

Directions downtown

Take _____ bus line 88, and then the 93.

_____ the 88 at the corner.

_____ at Third Street and Main Street.

_____ the 93 across the street.

Look at the _____ _____ for the time.

Use _____ or the correct change. Good luck.

tokens
get off
get on
catch
take
transfer
bus schedule

LISTEN

Tan talks to the bus driver.

UNDERSTAND   *Circle True, False, or We don't know.*

1. There are many people in the bus.   True   False   We don't know.
2. All the seats aren't full.   True   False   We don't know.
3. Tan can't wait for the next bus.   True   False   We don't know.

WRITE   *Fill in the missing parts of the dialog.*

Passenger: _____?

   Driver: Yes, it does. It stops at the adult school, but it's very crowded.

_____!

Passenger: I can't wait. I'm late for my class now!

   Driver: OK, get on.

Passenger: _____?

   Driver: It's fifty cents or a token.

WRITE   *Put the sentences of the dialog in the correct order. Write the numbers 1 to 8 in front of the sentences.*

_____ You can get on the 158 across the street.

_____ Take the bus line 158.

_____ Sure, what can I do for you?

_____ I don't know. Let's look at this bus schedule.

___/___ Can you help me?

_____ Where can I catch it?

_____ How can I get to the airport?

_____ How often does it run?

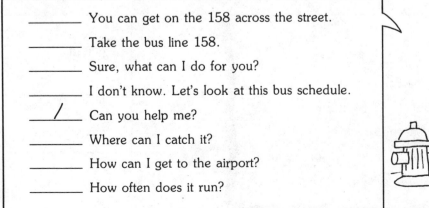

PAIR PRACTICE

Fold the page in half. Look at one side only.

Student 1	Student 2

Student 1

Listen to the questions and find the answers in the work schedule below.

A–OK ELECTRIC COMPANY
Daily Work Schedule
Day: *Monday*
For: *Mario Corral*

8 a.m. *pick up some new*
9 a.m. *electrical equipment*
at the airport and
10 a.m. *drop it off at the new*
shopping center downtown
11 a.m.

12 noon *have lunch*

1 p.m.
go to Long Beach, check
2 p.m. *and replace some light*
3 p.m. *bulbs in a pharmacy*
at 7364 Long Beach Blvd.
4. p.m. *Take the 405 freeway at*
5 p.m. *5th St. — and get off at*
Long Beach Blvd.

Now you ask these questions.

1. What kind of schedule is this?
2. What program can you watch at half past six?
3. What program is on T.V. at 9 p.m.?
4. What program is on at a quarter to eleven?
5. What time does the local news begin?
6. What time does the national news finish?
7. How many different programs are there on T.V. tonight?
8. How many movies are there on T.V. tonight?
9. Is there an educational program?
10. What is the name of the late movie?

FOLD HERE

Student 2

Ask these questions.

1. What kind of schedule is this?
2. Where does Mario pick up the electrical equipment?
3. Where does he drop off the equipment?
4. Where does he go after lunch?
5. Where's the pharmacy?
6. What freeway does he take?
7. Where does he get on the freeway?
8. Where does he get off the freeway?
9. What's the address of the pharmacy?
10. What time can Mario stop work?

Now you listen to the questions and find the answers in the T.V. program schedule below.

T.V. TONIGHT
PROGRAM SCHEDULE   CHANNEL 6

Time	Program
6:30 p.m.	Local News
7:00	National News
7:30	Learn English at Home
8:00	Movie: "A Story of Love"
10:00	Special Program: "Money and You"
11:00	News
11:30	The Late Movie: "The People Upstairs"

PHONICS   Long Vowels with Final Silent *e*

- *We often spell long vowels with two vowels: one vowel before one or more consonants with a silent **e** at the end of the word.*

- *Some exceptions are **have**, **live**, and **come.***

LISTEN   *Listen to the long vowels.*

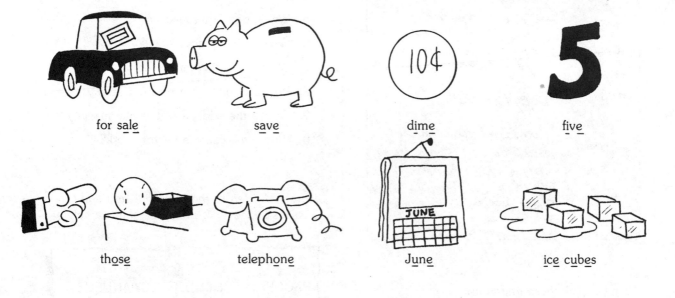

for s<u>a</u>l<u>e</u>   s<u>a</u>v<u>e</u>   d<u>i</u>m<u>e</u>   f<u>i</u>v<u>e</u>

th<u>o</u>s<u>e</u>   teleph<u>o</u>n<u>e</u>   J<u>u</u>n<u>e</u>   <u>i</u>c<u>e</u> c<u>u</u>b<u>e</u>s

LISTEN   *Listen to the three words. Circle the words that have the long vowel sounds with a silent final **e.***

1. can	(late)	chalk		6. thank	page	class
2. sit	pile	six		7. truck	number	cube
3. plus	but	June		8. drive	it	first
4. map	take	glasses		9. wall	date	that
5. line	single	dictionary		10. lot	home	problem

WRITE   *Fill in the spaces with **i** or **a** and the final silent **e.***

1. The d__t__ book with n__n__ p__g__s and f__v__ l__n__s costs only a d__m__.

2. R__d__ the bus to the big s__l__ and s__v__ money.

3. Don't t__k__ your w__f__ to a n__c__ dinner l__t__.

Are You Using This Ladder?

COMPETENCIES	• **Describing Basic Home and Work Activities**
GRAMMAR	• **The Present Continuous**
	• **The Future with *going to***
VOCABULARY	• **Verbs for Common Work and Home Activities**
SPELLING	• **Doubling Consonants**
	• **Deleting Silent Letters**

LISTEN

Joe Babcock is talking to Maria at work.

Joe: How are you doing,* Maria?

Maria: Pretty good, and you?

Joe: Just fine. Are you using this ladder?

Maria: No, I'm not. You can take it.

Joe: Thanks. What are you doing?

Maria: I'm cleaning this machine. This gear isn't turning. And what are you doing?

Joe: I'm helping the boss. He's fixing the air conditioners. It's hard, but we're trying.

Maria: Aren't they working?

Joe: Yes, they are, but they aren't working very well.

Maria: Do you need my help?

Joe: Sure, we can use a hand.

Maria: I can help you in a minute. I'm finishing up. Look! The gear's turning now.

UNDERSTAND   Circle True, False, or We don't know.

1. Maria is using the ladder.	True	False	We don't know.
2. Maria needs help.	True	False	We don't know.
3. Joe is helping Maria.	True	False	We don't know.
4. The gear isn't working.	True	False	We don't know.
5. The air conditioners are broken.	True	False	We don't know.
6. "How are you doing?" means "How are you?"	True	False	We don't know.

---

*   Pronounced "How ya doing'?" or "Howr ya doin'?"

GRAMMAR   The Present Continuous Tense

- *Use the present continuous to describe an action that is happening* **now.**

- *We form the present continuous with the verb* **to be (am, is, are)** *and the present participle* *(−***ing** *form) of the main verb.*

- *Do not use these verbs describing mental or physical conditions in the continuous:* **want, like, need, know, believe, see, hear.**

EXAMPLES

Question Form

How	**are**	you	**doing?**
	Are	you	**using this?**
	Is	it	**turning?**
	Aren't	they	**working?**

Affirmative

I	**'m**	**cleaning**	this gear.
He	**'s**	**fixing**	the air conditioners.
We	**'re**	**trying.**	
The gear	**is**	**turning**	now.

Negative

I	**'m not**	**using**	the ladder.
It	**isn't**	**turning.**	
They	**aren't**	**working**	very well.

Short Answers

Are you using this?	**Yes, I am.**	or	**No, I'm not.**
Is it turning?	**Yes, it is.**	or	**No, it isn't.**
Is Maria talking?	**Yes, she is.**	or	**No, she isn't.**
Is Joe standing?	**Yes, he is.**	or	**No, he isn't.**
Are they working?	**Yes, they are.**	or	**No, they aren't.**

READ   *Make complete sentences with the words in the box below.*

I	'm	speaking	now.
The boss	'm not	helping him	right now.
The gear	's (is)	fixing the machine	at this time.
Maria	isn't	turning	at this moment.
Joe	are	working	at this second.
The air conditioners	aren't	cleaning a gear	

LISTEN

Joe Babcock is giving Maria a factory tour.

> *Joe:* The air conditioners are on the roof. Meet me there.
>
> *Maria:* Wait. I don't know the way. Remember, I'm new here.
>
> *Joe:* Come on. Let me give you a tour. This is the receiving area. That's John. He's unloading some crates. And that's the main work area. All these people are making electronic parts.
>
> *Maria:* What's that woman doing?
>
> *Joe:* Oh, that's Esther. She works in the laboratory. She's testing some small parts. She's wearing a special uniform. Now, we're in the packing department. Linda's checking the parts. Joan's packing them in these cartons. Claudine's closing, taping, and stacking the cartons. Bill's loading the cartons on the truck.
>
> *Maria:* Look, there's Tan Tran.
>
> *Joe:* Where? I can't see him.
>
> *Maria:* He's standing next to the time clock. He's holding his lunch box. He's putting his time card in the time clock.
>
> *Joe:* Is he punching out and going home so soon?
>
> *Maria:* Yes, he is. He starts very early in the morning.

UNDERSTAND   *Circle True, False, or We don't know.*

1. Joe is a new employee.	True	False	We don't know.
2. The factory makes T.V. and radio parts.	True	False	We don't know.
3. Maria works in the packing department.	True	False	We don't know.
4. Tan eats lunch at work.	True	False	We don't know.
5. The time clock is in the laboratory.	True	False	We don't know.
6. Tan is starting work.	True	False	We don't know.

WRITE   *Underline all the verbs in the present continuous in the dialog above.*

PAIR PRACTICE   *Talk with another student about the pictures below.*

Student 1: What .... doing?
Student 2: He/She/They ....

John

Esther

Linda

Joan

Claudine

Bill

Tan

employees

Maria

Joe

the boss

the manager

PAIR PRACTICE   *Talk with another student about the pictures above.*

Student 1: What .... using?
Student 2: He/She/They .... using ....

LISTEN

Wanda is inviting Maria to a party.

Wanda: Hello, Maria? This is Wanda. How are you doing?

Maria: Fine. What about you?

Wanda: I'm busy. What are you doing?

Maria: I'm doing the housework, but I can't get any help. Mario's lying on the sofa; he isn't feeling very well. Theresa's writing a letter to my aunt and uncle. They're coming here for a visit soon. José's making a mess. It's raining and the dog and cat are running in and out. What about you? What are you doing?

Wanda: I'm getting ready for a party on Saturday afternoon. Can you come?

Maria: Sure, if it isn't raining.

UNDERSTAND   *Circle **True**, **False**, or **We don't know**.*

1. It is Wednesday.	True	False	We don't know.
2. "Housework" and "homework" are the same.	True	False	We don't know.
3. Maria is getting ready for a party.	True	False	We don't know.
4. Maria and Wanda have to do lots of things.	True	False	We don't know.

WRITE   *Underline all the present continuous verbs in the dialog above.*

PAIR PRACTICE   *Ask and answer questions about the picture above. Use short answers.*

Student 1: Is/Are ....?

Student 2: Yes,.............. / No, ...

WRITE   *Fill in the blanks with the correct form of the present continuous.*

Maria: What (1)_____ your family _____ ?
                                                do

Wanda: Stephen (2)_____ _____ in the garage.
                                    work

He (3)_____ _____ the garage door.
              fix

My son (4)_____ _____ T.V.
                      watch

My daughter (5)_____ _____ with some friends.
                              play

They (6)_____ _____ to records, and they (7)_____ _____ a mess.
              listen   make

The cats (8)_____ _____ upstairs.
                    sleep

And, I (9)_____ _____ break.
                take

I (10)_____ _____ some tea, and I (11)_____ _____ to you.
          drink   talk

DICTATION   *Cover the sentence under the line. Write the dictation,*
                 and then check your writing.

Dear Uncle Pedro and Aunt Alicia,

1. _____

   I'm not doing very much.

2. _____

   It's raining.

3. _____

   We're all staying at home today.

4. _____

   My mom is working in the kitchen, and my dad isn't feeling very well.

5. _____

   My mother is calling me now.

6. _____

   I know the housework is waiting for me!   Theresa

READ

Wanda and Stephen Bratko are having a party in the backyard.

PAIR PRACTICE   *Talk with another student about the picture above.*

Student 1: What .... doing?
Student 2: He/she/they ....
Student 1: Is/are ....?
Student 2: Yes, ... / No, ...

WRITE   *Put the sentences of the dialog in the correct order. Write the numbers 1 to 8 in front of the sentences.*

_____	He's cooking. I mean he's trying.
_____	She's talking with some friends.
_1_	What are you doing?
_____	And what about Stephen? What's he doing?
_____	Oh! They're playing with the cat and dog.
_____	And the kids?
_____	I'm looking at the people next door.
_____	Well, tell me. What's Wanda doing?

WRITE   *Answer the questionnaire.*

QUESTIONNAIRE

1. Are you taking any courses at any school?

   _____

2. What are you studying?

   _____

3. Why are you taking this course?

   _____

4. What kind of book are you using in your class?

   _____

5. Are you using a second book in your class?

   _____

6. Are you doing all the exercises in this book?

   _____

7. Are you filling out this questionnaire at school or at home?

   _____

READ

Maria and Wanda are talking at the party.

Wanda: What are you going to do tomorrow?

Maria: My Aunt Alicia and Uncle Pedro are going to arrive here from New York. I'm going to go to the airport and pick them up. They're going to stay with us. Then they're going to Mexico and visit my family.

Wanda: Are they going to be here long?

Maria: No, they aren't. They're going to stay only a few days.

Wanda: That's great!

Maria: This is a nice party, Wanda. Can I help you clean up?

Wanda: No, thanks. Stephen's going to help and so are the kids.

UNDERSTAND   Circle **True**, **False**, or **We don't know.**

1. Aunt Alicia and Uncle Pedro live in New York.	True	False	We don't know.
2. They're from Mexico.	True	False	We don't know.
3. Maria's from Mexico.	True	False	We don't know.
4. Maria's going to help Wanda clean up.	True	False	We don't know.

WRITE   *Underline **going to** in all the sentences in the dialog above.*

GRAMMAR   **The Future with *going to***

- *We use **going to** to express a future time.*

- *We use the present form of **to be** before **going**, and an infinitive after it.*

- *In speech we sometimes pronounce **going to** as **gonna**.*

EXAMPLES		to be		Infinitive	
My aunt and uncle		are	going	to arrive	tomorrow.
I		'm	going	to go	to the airport.
They		're	going	to be	here a few days.
Stephen		's	going	to help	me.

READ   *Make complete sentences with the words in the box below.*

Wanda	am			arrive	
I	am not			help Wanda	tomorrow.
They	is			clean up	after the party.
Stephen	isn't	going to		stay	a few days.
The kids	are			go to the airport	next week.
We	aren't			be here	soon.
Maria				fly to Mexico	

PAIR PRACTICE   *Talk with another student.*

Student 1: What .... going to do tomorrow?
Student 2: .... going to ....

1. Maria and Mario/
   go to the airport

2. Aunt Alicia and Uncle
   Pedro/visit their family

3. Wanda/rest

4. Stephen/watch football

5. kids/go to a movie

6. Wanda/call Maria

PAIR PRACTICE   *Talk with another student. Use the phrases below.*

Student 1: What are you going to do ....?
Student 2: I'm going to ....

1. tomorrow
2. tonight
3. tomorrow morning
4. tomorrow afternoon
5. tomorrow evening

6. next weekend
7. next week
8. next month
9. next year
10. ....

WRITE   *Fill in your schedule for tomorrow. Complete the sentences.*

1. _____ tomorrow morning.

2. _____ tomorrow afternoon.

3. _____ tomorrow evening.

4. _____ next weekend.

PAIR PRACTICE   *Fold this page in half. Look at one side only.*

Student 1

Listen to the questions and find the answers in the picture below.

Now you ask these questions.

1. Is Mario standing?
2. Is he working?
3. Why is he lying on the sofa?
4. Are the kids playing in the room?
5. Is Mario sleeping?
6. Is it nice outside?
7. What kind of day is it?
8. What program is on T.V.?

Student 2

Ask these questions.

1. Is Maria sitting?
2. Where's she standing?
3. What time is it?
4. Is she coming to work or going home?
5. What's she doing with her time card?
6. Is she fixing the time clock?
7. What's she wearing?
8. What's she holding?

Now you listen to the questions and find the answers in the picture below.

FOLD HERE

SPELLING   Doubling Consonants and Deleting Silent Letters

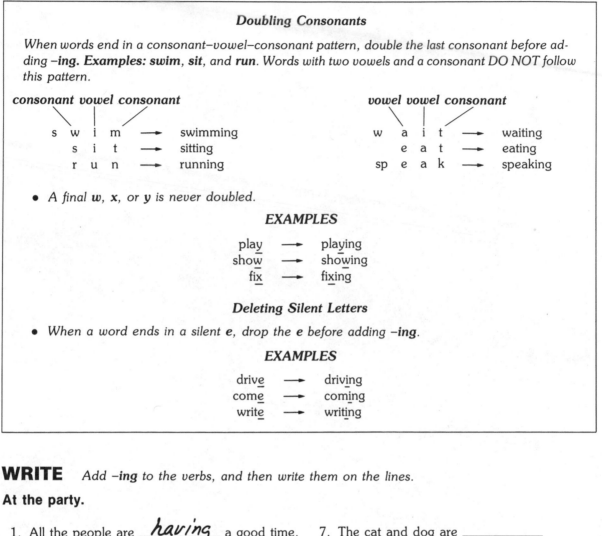

Doubling Consonants

When words end in a consonant–vowel–consonant pattern, double the last consonant before adding –ing. Examples: swim, sit, and run. Words with two vowels and a consonant DO NOT follow this pattern.

consonant vowel consonant

s w i m ⟶ swimming
s i t ⟶ sitting
r u n ⟶ running

vowel vowel consonant

w a i t ⟶ waiting
e a t ⟶ eating
sp e a k ⟶ speaking

- *A final **w**, **x**, or **y** is never doubled.*

EXAMPLES

play ⟶ playing
show ⟶ showing
fix ⟶ fixing

Deleting Silent Letters

- *When a word ends in a silent **e**, drop the **e** before adding –ing.*

EXAMPLES

drive ⟶ driving
come ⟶ coming
write ⟶ writing

WRITE   *Add –ing to the verbs, and then write them on the lines.*

At the party.

1. All the people are __*having*__ a good time.
   have

2. Maria and Wanda are _____.
   speak

3. Theresa's _____ in the swimming pool.
   swim

4. Wanda's _____ a plate.
   take

5. Mario is _____ Maria a hamburger.
   give

6. Maria is _____ a hamburger.
   get

7. The cat and dog are _____
   run

8. The boys are _____ over the fence.
   look

9. José is _____ outside.
   play

10. Maria isn't _____ the chair.
    use

11. Stephen is _____ a chair.
    fix

13

We Can't Find Our Luggage

COMPETENCIES	• Showing Possession
	• Filling out a Claim Form
	• Trying on Clothes
GRAMMAR	• The Possessive of Nouns
	• Possessive Adjectives and Pronouns
	• *too* + Adjective
VOCABULARY	• Clothing
	• Common Descriptive Adjectives
PHONICS	• The *j* Sound (as in *job*)

LISTEN

Maria is meeting her relatives, Pedro and Alicia Lopez, at the airport.

    Maria: Welcome! We're glad you're here.
    Alicia: Oh, it's great to see you again.
    Pedro: We're happy to be here.
    Mario: Let's get your relatives' luggage.

    Pedro: Our luggage isn't here!
Passenger: My bags are missing, too!
Passenger: Mine, too!
    Pedro: Let's go to the Lost and Found.

Pedro explains the problem to the baggage clerk.

    Pedro: Excuse me, we're Mr. and Mrs. Lopez. We can't find our luggage from Flight
              158, and he's missing his, too.
    Clerk: Whose bag is this? Is this yours? It's from your flight.
    Pedro: No, it doesn't belong to me. Mine is an old beige suit bag.
    Clerk: Is it your wife's bag?
    Pedro: No, it isn't her luggage. Hers is a large blue suitcase. Maybe it's his bag.
    A man: No, it isn't. My baggage is black. Maybe it's their bag.

UNDERSTAND   *Circle **True**, **False**, or **We don't know**.*

1. Three bags are missing.	True	False	We don't know.
2. The bag at the Lost and Found doesn't belong to Mr. and Mrs. Lopez.	True	False	We don't know.
3. Mr. and Mrs. Lopez can't find two bags.	True	False	We don't know.
4. "Luggage" and "baggage" mean the same.	True	False	We don't know.

GRAMMAR   The Possessive Case, Possessive Adjectives, and Possessive Pronouns

- *Possessive adjectives and pronouns express ownership, belonging, or a similar relation.*

Possessive Adjectives

Where are	**my**	bags?
It's from	**your**	flight.
Maybe it's	**his**	bag.
It isn't	**her**	luggage.
We can't find	**our**	luggage.
Maybe it's	**their**	bag.

Possessive Pronouns

	Mine	is an old beige suit bag.
Is this	**yours**	?
	His	is missing, too.
	Hers	is a large blue suitcase.
These are	**ours**	.
They can't find	**theirs**	.

- *We form the possessive case by adding an apostrophe and −s ('s) to the singular of most nouns, proper nouns, and irregular plurals. Add an apostrophe (') alone to plurals that end in −s.*

Possessive of Nouns

Singular:	Is it your	**wife's**	bag?
Plural:	Let's get your	**relatives'**	luggage.

READ   *Make complete sentences with the words and expressions in the box below.*

	my	bags,			mine	
This is	your	luggage,			yours	
These are	his	baggage,	but	where's	his	?
That's	her	suitcase,		where are	hers	
Those are	our	suit bags,			ours	
	their	handbag,			theirs	

PAIR PRACTICE

Talk with another student about the picture below. Use possessive adjectives.

Student 1: Whose .... is this?
Student 2: It's his/her/their ....

Mr. and Mrs. Lopez   Mrs. Snow   Mr. George Lodge   Mr. and Mrs. Brown

PAIR PRACTICE

Talk with another student about the picture above. Use the possessive pronouns.

Student 1: Whose .... is this?
Student 2: It's ....

REVIEW

Talk with another student about the picture above. Use object pronouns: **him**, **her**, *and* **them.**

Student 1: Who does the .... belong to?
Student 2: It belongs to ....

READ

Pedro: Our luggage isn't here!

Clerk: You can make a claim. What's in your luggage?

Alicia: There are three women's blouses, two skirts, a light blue coat, an orange sweater, seven pieces of underwear, some cosmetics, and four gifts.

Pedro: There are three pairs of pants, five shirts, a brown jacket, a suit, a black belt, six pairs of socks, a yellow tie, and seven pieces of underwear.

Clerk: Please fill out this baggage claim form.

WRITE   *Fill out the form for Mr. and Mrs. Lopez.*

BAGGAGE CLAIM FORM

Name: <u>Pedro and Alicia Lopez</u>   Date: <u>Oct. 23</u>

Airline: <u>Speedy Airlines</u>   Flight Number: <u>158</u>

From: <u>Dallas</u>   to <u>Los Angeles</u>

Number	Item	Number	Item

LISTEN

Alicia and Pedro are trying on some of Maria's and Mario's clothes.

Alicia: Let's try on these clothes. Try on this striped jacket.
Pedro: It doesn't fit; it's too tight.
Alicia: Try on these solid-colored pants.
Pedro: They're too long and loose. I can wear them for Halloween.
Alicia: Good idea. Halloween's tomorrow. Why don't you try on this short-sleeved shirt?
Pedro: It's not too bad. It fits fine.

UNDERSTAND   *Circle **True**, **False**, or **We don't know**.*

1. The striped jacket is too small.	True	False	We don't know.
2. The pants are one color.	True	False	We don't know.
3. Pedro likes the short-sleeved shirt.	True	False	We don't know.
4. Halloween is an American holiday.	True	False	We don't know.

WRITE   *Underline the word **too** in all the sentences in the dialog above.*

GRAMMAR   *too* + Adjective

- **Too** + **adjective** shows that something is excessive or more than sufficient. It has a negative result. It is different from **very**.

  EXAMPLES

The striped jacket is	**too tight.**	Results: I can't wear it/them.
The pants are	**too long.**	
They are	**too loose.**	
It's not	**too bad.**	

PAIR PRACTICE   *Talk with another student about the pictures below.*

Student 1: How does/do .... fit?
Student 2: Not well. It/They .... too ....
            or
            It's/They're not too bad.

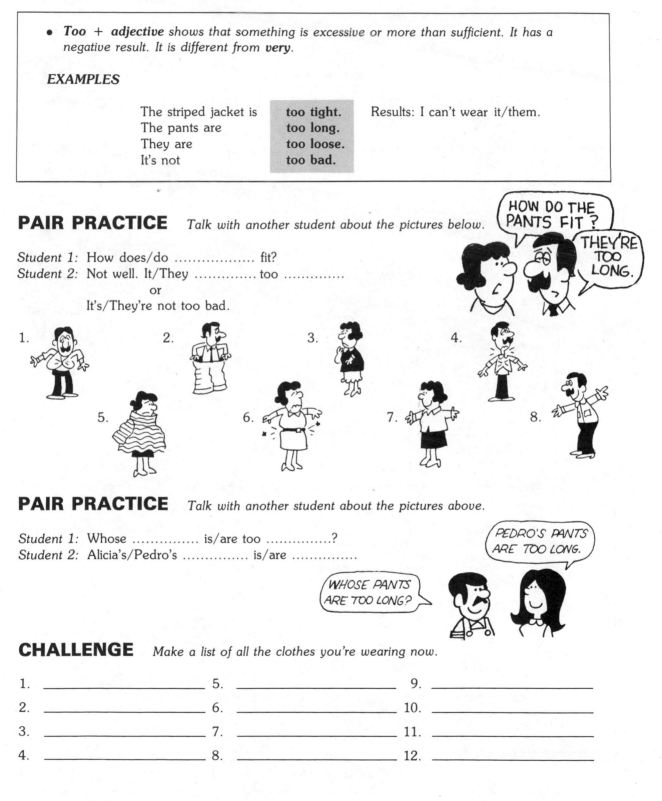

1. 2. 3. 4.

5. 6. 7. 8.

PAIR PRACTICE   *Talk with another student about the pictures above.*

Student 1: Whose .... is/are too ....?
Student 2: Alicia's/Pedro's .... is/are ....

CHALLENGE   *Make a list of all the clothes you're wearing now.*

1. _____	5. _____	9. _____
2. _____	6. _____	10. _____
3. _____	7. _____	11. _____
4. _____	8. _____	12. _____

LISTEN

The clerk is calling about the luggage.

WRITE

Fill in the spaces with the possessive pronouns: **mine, yours, his, hers, ours, theirs.** *The words under the lines are your clues.*

Alicia: Let's look at the clothes inside the bags. _____ are here.
my clothes

What about _____?
your clothes

Pedro: _____ are here, too.
my clothes

Alicia: Maria and Mario, come here! We have presents for you and the kids.

These are _____.
your presents

Maria: These are _____! Thank you very much.
mine and Mario's presents

Alicia: Here are the kids' presents. This is _____ and this
Theresa's present

is _____. I hope they like them.
José's present.

DICTATION

Cover the sentence under the line. Write the dictation, then check your writing.

Dear Pedro,

1. _____
   It's nice here with Maria's family.

2. _____
   We have our luggage now, and the presents, too.

3. _____
   The kids are playing with their presents now.

4. _____
   We're having a very good time.

5. _____
   See you next week.

   Mom and Dad

To: Pedro Lopez
9505 River St.
Dallas, Texas
     75265

WRITE   *Fill in the spaces with **your** or **you're**. Remember that **you're** means **you are** and **your** is possessive.*

Theresa: Hey, Mom, _you're_ very funny. Where are you going?

Maria: I'm going to the Halloween party with you and _____ brother. _____ clothes are pretty funny, too.

Theresa: You can't go with us. _____ too old!

Maria: Maybe I am, but you and _____ brother can't go out alone on Halloween night. It's too dangerous. Where are _____ bags?

José: Here they are. Let's go!

PAIR PRACTICE   *Talk with another student about the picture below.*

Student 1: What's .... wearing?
Student 2: He/She is wearing ....

Theresa   José   Maria

GROUP ACTIVITY

Find the students with the following clothes on the previous page. Write their names in the spaces below.

1. _____
   is wearing a blue blouse.

2. _____
   is wearing a loose shirt.

3. _____
   is wearing a short–sleeved shirt.

4. _____
   is wearing a long–sleeved shirt.

5. _____
   is wearing a tie.

6. _____
   is wearing green socks.

7. _____
   is wearing brown shoes.

8. _____
   is wearing a white belt.

9. _____
   is wearing an old hat.

10. _____
    is wearing blue pants.

11. _____
    is wearing a solid–colored jacket.

12. _____
    is wearing glasses.

DISCUSSION

How many differences in clothes can you find in the pictures below?

PHONICS   The *j* sound

> - The *j* sound is usually spelled *j* at the beginning of a word.
> - It is sometimes spelled *g* before *e*, *i*, or *y*.
> - At the end of a word, it is spelled *g* before final *e*.

LISTEN

January   job   Japan   juice

dangerous   gym   package   baggage

LISTEN   Listen to three words. Circle the words that have the *j* sound.

1. get   (baggage)   eight
2. join   again   English
3. night   belong   July
4. glad   bag   damage
5. begin   glasses   danger

6. give   juice   game
7. orange   flight   good
8. gifts   go   large
9. jacket   light   long
10. get   single   join

WRITE   Fill in the blanks with *j* or *g*.

1. There's a lar_g_e _j_acket in a packa____e in the gara____e.

2. I drink a lot of oran____e ____uice in ____une and ____uly.

3. I have a dan____erous ____ob in ____apan in ____anuary.

Who Are These People?

COMPETENCIES	• **Understanding Family Relationships**
	• **Buying Furniture**
	• **Reading Newspaper Want Ads**
GRAMMAR	• **The Possessive with** *of*
VOCABULARY	• **Names of Relatives**
	• **Common Descriptive Adjectives**
PHONICS	• **The** *s* **Sound**

LISTEN

Nancy Barns and her son, Bobby, are looking at a photo album.

Nancy: What are you doing?

Bobby: I'm looking at one of the family photo albums, but I don't know some of the people in the pictures. Are most of them members of the family?

Nancy: Yes, here's a picture of your grandparents, your father, and your sister, Patty.

Bobby: Oh, I know them. But what about the people in the next picture? Are both of them relatives, too?

Nancy: No, they aren't. That's Ann Porter and her husband. They're good friends of mine. They're the owners of the apartment building down the street. And this is our family tree. Let me explain this to you. These two people are David and his wife, Carol. They're my brother-in-law and sister-in-law. They're your uncle and aunt.

Bobby: Are Patty and I their niece and nephew?

Nancy: That's right.

Bobby: What's the relationship between Eric and me?

Nancy: You're cousins. Now do you understand?

Bobby: It's complicated, but I think I understand.

UNDERSTAND   *Circle True, False, or We don't know.*

1. There's only one photo album.   True   False   We don't know.
2. Ann Porter is a member of the family.   True   False   We don't know.
3. Nancy and Carol come from the same family.   True   False   We don't know.
4. Bobby and Eric are relatives.   True   False   We don't know.

WRITE   *Underline the word **of** in all the sentences in the dialog above.*

READ

PAIR PRACTICE   *Talk with another student about the pictures below.*

Student 1: Who does .... look like?
Student 2: .... looks like his/her ....

1. Dad   father   2. Nancy   mother   3. Bobby   father

4. Patty   mother   5. Roy   brother   6. Nancy   sister

PAIR PRACTICE   *Talk with another student.*

Student 1: Do you look like your ....?
Student 2: Yes, I do./No, I don't.

1. mother   6. aunt
2. father   7. sister
3. grandfather   8. brother
4. grandmother   9. cousin
5. uncle   10. ....

READ

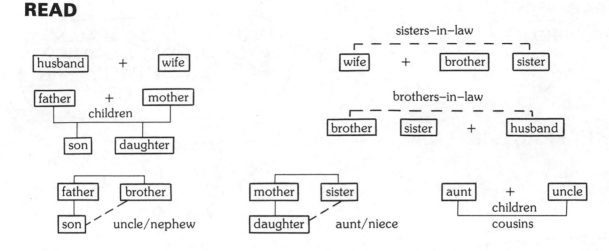

WRITE   *Fill in the blanks with the words above.*

Do you mean my cousin's father is my (1) __*uncle*__ and

my uncle's wife is my (2) _____ and

my aunt's children are my (3) _____ and

my father's mother is my (4) _____ and

my mother's father is my (5) _____ and

my grandparents' son is my (6) _____?

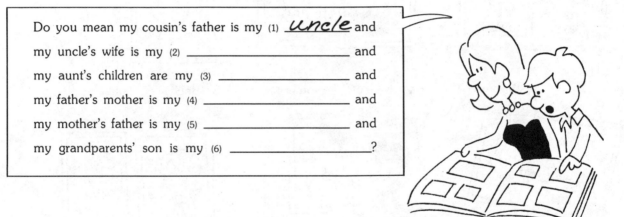

Yes, dear, that's right. And, my uncle and (7)_____'s

daughter is my cousin, and my brother and (8)_____'s

kids are my niece and nephew, and my (9)_____'s

sister is my sister-in-law, and my (10)_____'s husband

is my brother-in-law, and you are my (11)_____,

and I am your (12)_____!

PAIR PRACTICE   *Talk with another student about the family tree below.*

Student 1: What's the relationship between ....?
Student 2: They're .... and ....

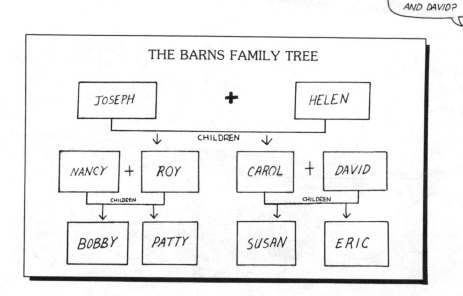

THE BARNS FAMILY TREE

JOSEPH + HELEN

CHILDREN

NANCY + ROY   CAROL + DAVID

CHILDREN   CHILDREN

BOBBY   PATTY   SUSAN   ERIC

WHAT'S THE RELATIONSHIP BETWEEN CAROL AND DAVID?

THEY'RE HUSBAND AND WIFE.

PAIR PRACTICE   *Talk with another student about the family tree above.*

Student 1: What's the relationship between .... and ....?
Student 2: .... is ....'s ....

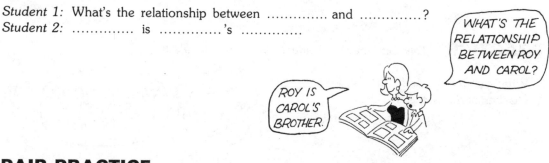

WHAT'S THE RELATIONSHIP BETWEEN ROY AND CAROL?

ROY IS CAROL'S BROTHER.

PAIR PRACTICE   *Talk with another student about the family tree above.*

Student 1: Who's ....(name).............'s ....?
Student 2: ....(name)........... is.

WHO'S ERIC'S FATHER?

DAVID IS.

WRITE   *Make your family tree. Fill in the appropriate spaces with the names of the members of your family. Add spaces if necessary.*

MY FAMILY TREE

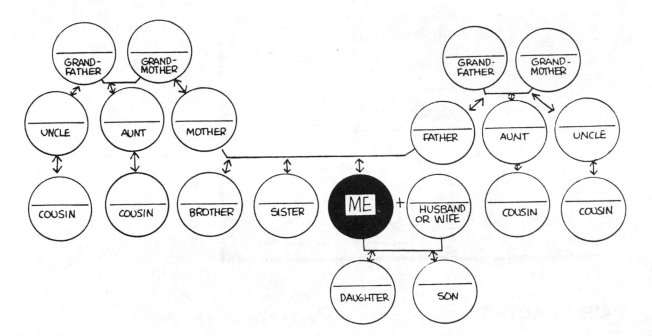

PAIR PRACTICE   *Talk with another student about your family tree.*

Student 1: What's your ....'s name?
Student 2: His/her name is ....

PAIR PRACTICE   *Talk with another student about your family tree.*

Student 1: Who's ....(name).............. ?
Student 2: That's my ....

GRAMMAR   *of*

- *Use an **of**–phrase to show ownership or association.*

EXAMPLES

They're good	friends	of mine.
They're	the owners	of the apartment building.
They're	members	of the family.

- *Use an **of**–phrase after a quantity word like **one**, **both**, **some**, and **most**.*

EXAMPLES

I'm looking at	one	of the photo albums.	
I don't know	some	of these people.	
Are	most	of them	relatives?
Are	both	of these people	relatives?

READ   *Make complete sentences with the words in the box below.*

Bobby				the photo album.
Nancy	is	a friend		the family.
Ann Porter		a member		an apartment building.
David		the owner	of	mine.
Carol	isn't	part		ours.
He		one		theirs.
She				hers.
				his.

PAIR PRACTICE   *Talk with another student. Describe the photo album pictures.*

Student 1: Is/Are .... in the pictures?
Student 2: In one of the pictures, ... is/are with a friend of ....

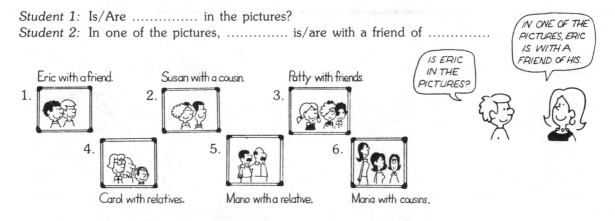

IS ERIC IN THE PICTURES?

IN ONE OF THE PICTURES, ERIC IS WITH A FRIEND OF HIS.

1. Eric with a friend.
2. Susan with a cousin.
3. Patty with friends.
4. Carol with relatives.
5. Mario with a relative.
6. Maria with cousins.

PAIR PRACTICE

Talk with another student about the pictures below. Use **one,** **some,** *or* **most.**

Student 1: Is/Are .... in all of the pictures?
Student 2: .... in one/some/most of them.

IS MARIO IN ALL OF THE PICTURES?

HE'S IN MOST OF THEM.

1.
Mario   Maria
Patty   Bobby

2.
Mario and Maria

3.
Mario and David

4.
Maria and Carol

5.
Maria, Mario
Carol and David

6.
Carol, David
Eric, Susan

WRITE   *Fill out the questionnaire.*

QUESTIONNAIRE

1. How many people are there in your family? _____

2. How many brothers and sisters do you have?

                    Number of brothers: _____

                    Number of sisters: _____

3. Do all the members of your family live together? _____

4. How many members of your family do you live with? _____

5. Do you live with both of your parents? _____

6. Are both of your parents living? _____

7. Are all of your grandparents living? _____

8. Do most of your relatives live outside this country? _____

9. How many of your relatives live in this country? _____

10. Do any of your relatives live near you? _____

PAIR PRACTICE   *Talk with another student.*

Student 1: Tell me about your family.
Student 2: My mother and father are ....
            I also have ....

TELL ME ABOUT YOUR FAMILY.

MY MOTHER AND FATHER ARE IN CHICAGO. I ALSO HAVE A BROTHER IN BOSTON.

LISTEN

Ann Porter's speaking to Nancy Barns on the telephone.

Ann: Hello, Nancy, this is Ann Porter. Do you want to go shopping with me to-day? I'm going to Vincent's Antique and Used Furniture Store. I need a refrigerator for one of my apartments.

Nancy: I'm sorry, I can't go today. But we have a used refrigerator in our garage, and it's for sale.

Ann: Oh, really? What type of refrigerator is it?

Nancy: It's a frost–free model.

Ann: What size is it?

Nancy: It's average size.

Ann: What color is it?

Nancy: White.

Ann: What condition is it in?

Nancy: It's in excellent condition.

Ann: How old is it?

Nancy: It's five or six years old.

Ann: How much is it?

Nancy: For you, real cheap!

Ann: Can I come and see it this afternoon?

Nancy: Sure, come over about two.

UNDERSTAND   *Circle True, False, or We don't know.*

1. Nancy is selling a new refrigerator.	True	False	We don't know.
2. It isn't too big or too small.	True	False	We don't know.
3. "What type?" means "What kind?"	True	False	We don't know.
4. Nancy is using the refrigerator.	True	False	We don't know.
5. "Real cheap" means "very cheap."	True	False	We don't know.

PAIR PRACTICE   *Ask and answer questions about the furniture in the picture.*

Student 1: What size/color/condition is the ....?
Student 2: It's ....

WRITE *What kinds of questions can Ann Porter ask the furniture salesperson? Help her make a list of questions.*

WRITE   *Fill in the spaces with the words from the box below.*

of this store	of them	of the refrigerators
of my apartments	of furniture	of the salespersons

Ann Porter: Excuse me, are you one (1)_____?

Mr. Vincent: No, I'm not. I'm the owner (2)_____. May I help you?

Ann Porter: I need a refrigerator for one (3)_____. I see

a lot (4)_____, but no refrigerators.

Mr. Vincent: Many (5)_____ are in the next room.

Ann Porter: Are most (6)_____ in good condition?

Mr. Vincent: All (7)_____ are in excellent condition.
Ann Porter: How much do they cost?
Mr. Vincent: They're $500.00 each.
Ann Porter: That's too expensive for a used refrigerator. Thanks anyway.
Mr. Vincent: You're welcome. Come back again soon.

WRITE   *Put the sentences of the dialog in the correct order. Write the numbers 1 to 8 in front of the sentences.*

_____ It sure is. How much is it?

_____ Sure, come in. It's in the garage.

_____ That's great. Here's a hundred dollars. See you tomorrow.

_____ That's a good price. When can I pick it up?

_____ Here it is. Isn't it in good condition?

_____ One hundred dollars.

__1__ Hi, Nancy, can I see your used refrigerator?

_____ What about tomorrow? Roy and I can help you move it.

PAIR PRACTICE   *Fold this page in half. Look at one side only.*

Student 1

Listen to the questions and find the answers in the newspaper ads below.

ANTIQUE DESK

Big, beautiful, brown antique
desk for only $500.00
Great condition
Call Mr. Welch at 987–2361.

TYPEWRITER

Small, used black and white
typewriter. Clean, 5 years
old. Works very well.
Only $75.00
Call Alice at 945–0932.

Now you ask these questions.

1. What kind of car is in the ad?
2. What color is the car?
3. How much is the car?
4. What condition is the car in?
5. How old is the car?
6. What size is the car?
7. What kind of truck is for sale?
8. What color is it?
9. How much is it?
10. What year is it?
11. Who is selling it?
12. What is his telephone number?

Student 2

Ask these questions.

1. What kind of desk is in the ad?
2. What color is the desk?
3. What size is the desk?
4. How much is the desk?
5. What condition is the desk in?
6. How old is the desk?
7. What kind of typewriter is in the ad?
8. What color is it?
9. What size it?
10. How old is it?
11. Who is selling it?
12. What is her telephone number?

Now you listen to the questions and find the answers in the newspaper ads below.

CAR

Small, blue sports car,
1979, good condition
Only $1200.00
Call Pat at 459–2398.

TRUCK

Large, brown 1958 truck,
needs repairs
$200.
Call Jack at 876–2639.

FOLD HERE

PHONICS   The s Sounds

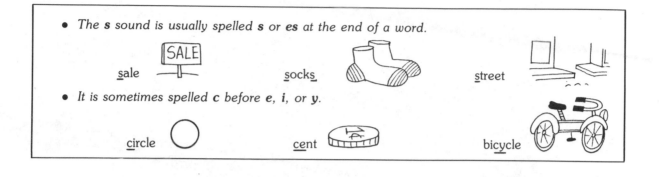

- The **s** sound is usually spelled **s** or **es** at the end of a word.

  <u>s</u>ale   <u>socks</u>   <u>s</u>treet

- It is sometimes spelled **c** before **e**, **i**, or **y**.

  <u>c</u>ircle   <u>c</u>ent   bi<u>c</u>ycle

LISTEN   Listen to the words. Circle the words that have the s sound.

1. (ice)   can   machine   6. back   shop   ask
2. call   false   child   7. picture   test   company
3. church   record   nursery   8. cup   city   watch
4. coin   teacher   this   9. piece   shoe   kitchen
5. English   correct   center   10. locker   correct   nurse

CROSSWORD   Fill in the crossword puzzle with the names for the objects below.

ACROSS   DOWN

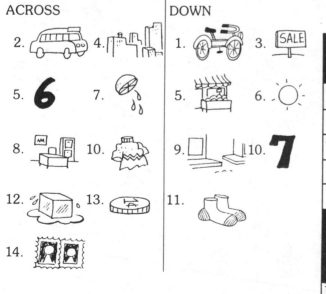

15

I Want You to Hire a Cleaning Crew

COMPETENCIES	• Telling Someone What to Do
GRAMMAR	• Verb + Infinitive
	• Verb + Object + Infinitive
	• *why*/*because*
	• The Simple Past
VOCABULARY	• Common Cleaning Items
	• Common Work Activities
	• *know how to*
PHONICS	• The /o/ Sound (as in *wash*)

LISTEN

Ann Porter is talking to Paul Green about her vacant apartment.

I WANT YOU TO HIRE A CLEANING CREW AND I WANT THEM TO CLEAN THE APARTMENT BEFORE MR. AND MRS. BOULOS MOVE IN.

Ann: Paul, do you have a minute?

Paul: Sure, why?

Ann: Because I want to* talk to you about the vacant apartment. I want you to hire a cleaning crew and I want them to clean the apartment before Mr. and Mrs. Boulos move in.

Paul: Do you want me to call a painter, too?

Ann: Yes, and I want them to paint every room.

Paul: What about the bathroom?

Ann: What's the matter with the bathroom?

Paul: There's a broken shower door, a cracked mirror, a damaged fan, a leaky toilet, and a clogged drain.

Ann: Don't you know how to repair them?

Paul: Well, I like to fix things, but that's a very big job. I don't know how. I don't have the skills.

Ann: I don't want to spend a lot of money.

Paul: I can ask the students at the adult school. Some of them have the skills and want to make extra money.

Ann: I like that idea. Try it.

UNDERSTAND   *Circle True, False, or We don't know.*

1. The apartment is in good condition.   True   False   We don't know.
2. There are problems in the kitchen.   True   False   We don't know.
3. Ann doesn't want to spend much money.   True   False   We don't know.
4. Paul wants to paint the apartment.   True   False   We don't know.
5. Ann likes to fix things.   True   False   We don't know.

---

* "Want to" is sometimes pronounced "wanna."

GRAMMAR   Infinitives

- We usually use an infinitive (**to** + the base form of the verb) after a verb (except modals).

EXAMPLES

	Verb	Infinitive	
I	want	to talk	to you.
I	like	to fix	things.
I	don't want	to spend	a lot of money.
Some of them	want	to make	extra money.
Do you	know how	to repair	them?

- We often place the object of the sentence between **want** and the infinitive.

EXAMPLES

	Verb	Object	Infinitive	
I	want	you	to get	a cleaning crew.
I	want	them	to clean	the apartment.
Do you	want	me	to get	a painter, too?
I	want	him	to paint	every room.

READ   Make complete sentences with the words in the boxes below.

Ann Porter	likes	to work.
Paul Green	doesn't like	to spend a lot of money.
Mona Boulos	want	to have a clean apartment.
The painter	doesn't want	to paint.
The cleaning crew	knows how	to fix things.
I	doesn't know how	to fix the sink.

Ann Porter		Ann Porter	to help.
Paul Green		Paul Green	to pay a lot of money.
The painter	want	the painter	to do a good job.
The cleaning crew		the cleaning crew	to call a painter.
I	wants	you	to paint every room.
She		her	to work.
He		him	to clean the apartment.
They		them	to be happy.

PAIR PRACTICE   *Talk with another student. Use the phrases below.*

Student 1: Do you know how ....?
Student 2: Yes, I do. / No, I don't.

1. to fix machines
2. to clean your home
3. to drive a car
4. to swim
5. to cook

6. to speak English
7. to paint
8. to tell time
9. to write
10. to ....

WRITE   *Fill in the questionnaire below.*

SKILLS QUESTIONNAIRE

What do you know how to do?

1. *I know how to speak English.* 3. _____
2. _____ 4. _____

What do you like to do?

1. _____ 3. _____
2. _____ 4. _____

What **don't** you know how to do, but want to learn to do?

1. _____ 3. _____
2. _____ 4. _____

What do you need to know for a good job in your occupation?

1. _____ 3. _____
2. _____ 4. _____

CHALLENGE   *What do you think employers want all of their employees to do?*

1. _____
2. _____
3. _____
4. _____
5. _____

PAIR PRACTICE   *Talk with another student. Use the pictures below.*

Student 1: What's the matter with the bathroom?
Student 2: There's ....

1. a leaky toilet
2. a damaged fan
3. a dirty floor
4. a broken shower door
5. a clogged drain
6. cracked paint
7. a cracked mirror
8. a broken window
9. a broken lock

PAIR PRACTICE   *Talk with another student.*

Student 1: What does Ann want .... to do?
Student 2: She wants .... to ....

Paul Green   the painter   the cleaning crew   a repairman   Mr. and Mrs. Boulos

PAIR PRACTICE   *Talk with another student. Ask questions using the phrases below.*

Student 1: Why does Ann want .... to ....?
Student 2: Because ....

1. Paul Green/fix the sink and toilet
2. the cleaning crew/clean the apartment
3. the painter/paint every room
4. Mr. and Mrs. Boulos/move in on December 1st
5. a repairman/fix the problems in the bathroom
6. Paul Green/ask some students at the adult school

LISTEN

David Fernandez and Sami Hamati are looking at the school bulletin board.

David: Look at this notice on the bulletin board. Paul Green's looking for people to fix some bathroom fixtures.

Sami: Let's apply for the job. What do you say? We have the experience to do it.

David: Why not? Let's talk to Paul about it.

> **WANTED:**
> **Repairman to fix**
> **bathroom fixtures.**
> **See Paul Green in**
> **the wood shop.**

David and Sami are speaking to Paul Green about the job.

David: Hi, Paul. We want to speak to you about your notice on the bulletin board. Sami and I want to apply for the job. We have the skills to do it.

Paul: When can you begin?

Sami: What about the weekend?

Paul: That sounds good. I have some money to buy some materials. What kind of supplies do you need to do the job?

David: We need some plumbing equipment to fix the toilet and the drains. We can make a list for you.

UNDERSTAND   *Circle True, False, or We don't know.*

1. Paul Green's notice is in the newspaper.   True   False   We don't know.
2. David and Sami can fix the problems.   True   False   We don't know.
3. Paul Green wants them to do the job.   True   False   We don't know.
4. David and Sami need some equipment.   True   False   We don't know.
5. Paul Green can pay them a lot of money.   True   False   We don't know.

GRAMMAR   The Use of the Infinitive to Show Purpose

- *We sometimes use an infinitive to show purpose.*

EXAMPLES

	Noun	*Infinitive*	
He's looking for	**a repairman**	**to fix**	some bathroom fixtures.
We have	**the skills**	**to do**	the job.
I have	**some money**	**to buy**	some materials.
They need	**some equipment**	**to fix**	the drains.

READ   *Make complete sentences with the words in the box below.*

David and Sami				
Paul Green	has	money	to buy	some supplies.
Ann Porter	have	supplies	to fix	the fixtures.
Mr. and Mrs.	needs	equipment	to pay	the rent.
Boulos	need	repairmen	to clean	the job.
The cleaning crew		the skills	to do	the apartment.

PAIR PRACTICE   *Talk with another student. Use the phrases below.*

Student 1: Do you have .... to ....?
Student 2: Yes, I do. / No, I don't.

1. money/buy supplies
2. money/buy new furniture
3. skills/find a job
4. equipment/fix a car
5. supplies/cook a big dinner

6. money/rent a house
7. skills/fix machines
8. friends/help you
9. supplies/clean your home
10. ....

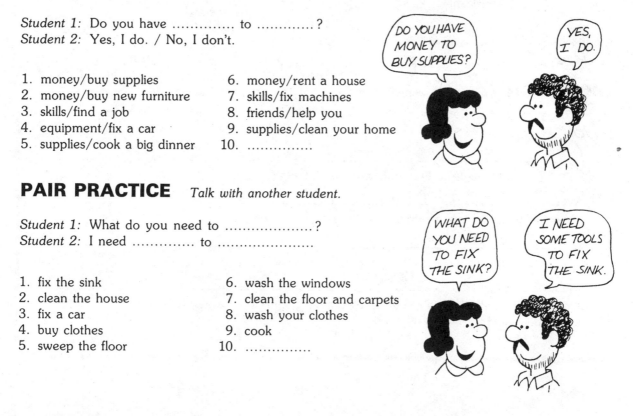

PAIR PRACTICE   *Talk with another student.*

Student 1: What do you need to ....?
Student 2: I need .... to ....

1. fix the sink
2. clean the house
3. fix a car
4. buy clothes
5. sweep the floor

6. wash the windows
7. clean the floor and carpets
8. wash your clothes
9. cook
10. ....

READ

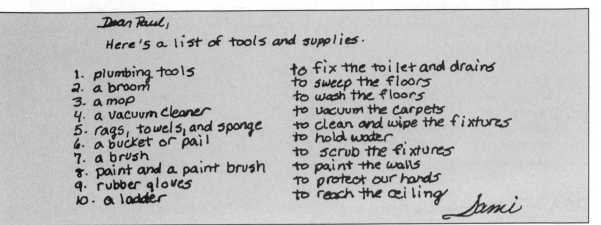

Dear Paul,

Here's a list of tools and supplies.

1.	plumbing tools	to fix the toilet and drains
2.	a broom	to sweep the floors
3.	a mop	to wash the floors
4.	a vacuum cleaner	to vacuum the carpets
5.	rags, towels, and sponge	to clean and wipe the fixtures
6.	a bucket or pail	to hold water
7.	a brush	to scrub the fixtures
8.	paint and a paint brush	to paint the walls
9.	rubber gloves	to protect our hands
10.	a ladder	to reach the ceiling

Sami

PAIR PRACTICE

Talk with another student. Ask questions using the pictures below. Answer in your own words.

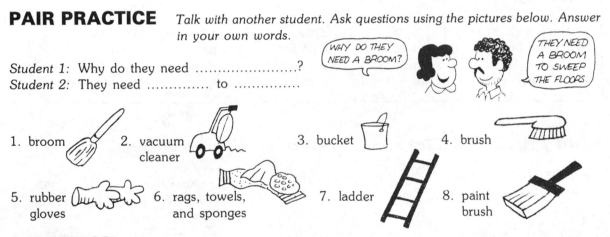

Student 1: Why do they need ....?
Student 2: They need .... to ....

WHY DO THEY NEED A BROOM?

THEY NEED A BROOM TO SWEEP THE FLOORS.

1. broom
2. vacuum cleaner
3. bucket
4. brush
5. rubber gloves
6. rags, towels, and sponges
7. ladder
8. paint brush

DICTATION

Cover the sentence under the line. Write the dictation, then check your writing.

Dear Ann,

1. _____

Two students from the adult school are doing the work.

2. _____

They need some materials and tools to do the job.

3. _____

Do you want me to buy them with my money?

5. _____

Don't worry about the tools. I'm borrowing some from a neighbor.

Paul Green

WRITE *Put the sentences of the dialog in the correct order. Write the numbers 1 to 8 in front of the sentences.*

_____ I want you to look at the living room door.

_____ Do you want me to fix the lock?

_____ I can try!

___1___ Oh, David, do you have a minute?

_____ It has a broken lock.

_____ Sure, what do you want?

_____ Yes, can you?

_____ What's the matter with the door?

WRITE *Fill in the spaces with the words in the box.*

Ann Porter and Paul Green are talking on the telephone.

Ann: How are the workers (1)____*doing*____?

Paul: Just fine. They're (2)_____ very hard.

Ann: Are they (3)_____ a good job?

Paul: Yes, they (4)_____. (5)_____ you have any free time?

Ann: I (6)_____ some free time after four o'clock today. Why?

Paul: I (7)_____ you (8)_____ come and look at the apartment. I think we (9)_____ (10)_____ before four.

Ann: That (11)_____ fast work! See you about four o'clock.

to
can
Do
are
have
's
want
doing
working
finish

READ

Paul Green is delivering more paint.

Paul: Did you do all the work?

Sami: No we didn't. We fixed the toilet and the drains, washed the windows and floors, vacuumed the carpet, and cleaned the fixtures, but we didn't finish the painting because we didn't have enough paint. I called you this morning and left a message on your answering machine.

Paul: I know. I just got your message. I went to the store and bought more paint. I came here right away. Here's the paint.

David: Great!

UNDERSTAND   *Circle True, False, or **We don't know.***

1. Sami and David finished all the work.	True	False	We don't know.
2. "Got your message" means "I received your message."	True	False	We don't know.
3. Paul bought two gallons of paint.	True	False	We don't know.
4. "Right away" means "immediately."	True	False	We don't know.

GRAMMAR   The Simple Past Tense

- *We add the* **–ed** *ending to form the past tense of regular verbs in the affirmative only. Do not use the* **–ed** *ending with verbs in the question and negative forms.*

- *The* **–ed** *ending is pronounced* **t, d,** *or* **id.**

EXAMPLES   *Affirmative*

We	**fixed**	the toilet and drains.
We	**washed**	the windows and floors.
We	**vacuumed**	the carpets.
We	**cleaned**	the fixtures.
I	**called**	you this morning.
I	**arrived**	home.

- *We use* **did** *to signal questions and* **did not** *to signal negatives.*

- ***Didn't*** *is a contraction of* **did not.**

EXAMPLES   *Question*   *Negative*

Did	you	**finish?**		We	**didn't finish.**	
Did	you	**do**	all the work?	We	**didn't have**	enough paint.

READ   *Make complete sentences with the words in the box below.*

We	fixed	
I	didn't fix	the work.
Paul	finished	the toilet.
He	didn't finish	Paul.
They	called	the drains.
Sami and David	didn't call	the walls.
	painted	
	didn't paint	

PAIR PRACTICE   *Talk with another student. Use the phrases below.*

Student 1: What did .... do?
Student 2: ....ed ....

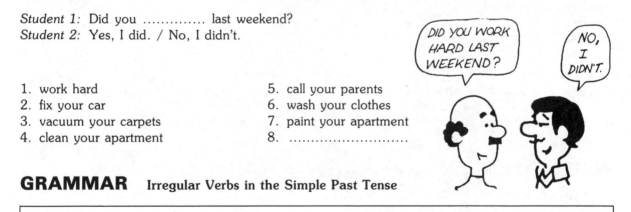

1. Sami and David / paint the walls
2. Sami / fix the toilet
3. David / vacuum the carpets
4. Sami / call Paul Green

5. Paul / arrive home
6. David / clean the fixtures
7. Sami / wash the windows
8. David and Sami / work hard

PAIR PRACTICE   *Talk with another student. Use the phrases below.*

Student 1: Did you .... last weekend?
Student 2: Yes, I did. / No, I didn't.

1. work hard
2. fix your car
3. vacuum your carpets
4. clean your apartment

5. call your parents
6. wash your clothes
7. paint your apartment
8. ....

GRAMMAR   Irregular Verbs in the Simple Past Tense

- *There are many irregular verb forms in the past tense. We use them in the affirmative only. Here are a few irregular verbs.*

Present Tense	Past Tense		EXAMPLES	
leave	left	I	**left**	a message.
get	got	I	**got**	your message.
buy	bought	I	**went**	to the store.
go	went	I	**bought**	some paint.
come	came	I	**came**	right away.

READ   *Make complete sentences with the words in the boxes below.*

What Who Where	did	Paul Sami they	do? buy? leave? come? get? go?

He They	went left bought got came did	to the house. some paint. to the store. a message. the work. right away.

PAIR PRACTICE   *Talk with another student using the phrases below.*

Student 1: What did .... do?
Student 2: ....(irregular   verb)..............

1. Sami and David / do the work
2. Sami / leave a message
3. Paul / get the message
4. Paul / go to the store
5. Paul / buy some paint
6. Paul / come right away

PAIR PRACTICE   *Talk with another student using the phrases below. Answer with short answers.*

Student 1: Did you ....?
Student 2: Yes, I did.
Student 1: When/what time did you ....?
Student 2: I ....

1. work yesterday
2. clean your apartment last weekend
3. call a friend or relative yesterday
4. come to school last night
5. go to the store last Saturday
6. buy a lot of food last week
7. arrive home late last night
8. do your homework yesterday

WRITE   *Fill in the spaces with the words in the box below.*

Paul Green is talking to Mrs. Ann Porter.

did	didn't	go	went

Paul: I ___*went*___ to the store to buy some paint.

Ann: _____ you _____ to the Maxwell's Hardware Store?

Paul: No, I _____ _____ there. I went to a department store.

Ann: Why _____ you _____ there?

Paul: I _____ there because paint is on sale this week.

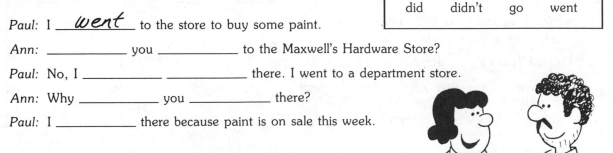

PAIR PRACTICE   *Fold the page in half. Look at one side only.*

Student 1	Student 2

Student 1

Listen to the questions and find the answers in the supply list below.

LIST OF SUPPLIES:

1. broom
2. mop
3. rags and sponges
4. tools
5. buckets
6. vacuum
7. paint brush
8. ladder
9. rubber gloves
10. brush
11. safety glasses
12. paper towels

Now ask these questions.

1. What room of the house is in the picture?
2. What's the matter with the sink?
3. What's the matter with the refrigerator?
4. Is the stove clean?
5. Is the window all right?
6. Are the walls in good condition?
7. What's the matter with the curtains?
8. What other problems are there?

Student 2

Ask these questions.

1. What do you use to clean windows?
2. What do you use to wash a car?
3. What do you use to protect your eyes?
4. What do you use to fix a broken door?
5. What do you need to replace a light on the ceiling?
6. What kinds of things do you need to clean a house?
7. Read the items in the list.

Now listen to the questions and find the answers in the picture below.

FOLD HERE

FOLD HERE

PHONICS   The /o/ Sound (as in *wash*)

- *We usually spell /o/ as* **o**. *We spell it as* **a** *before* **l** *and after* **w**. *This sound sometimes varies in different parts of the country.*

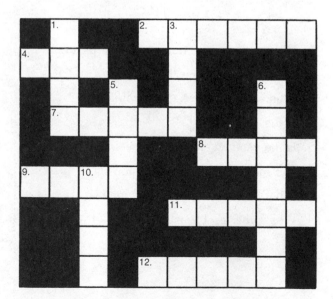

dog   lost   ball   wash

LISTEN   *Listen to the words. Circle the words that have the /o/ sound.*

1. (wash)   back   glasses   6. boss   too   over
2. map   tall   table   7. mop   chalk   scrub
3. lamp   wall   shop   8. at   man   small
4. wait   Sunday   talk   9. walk   father   pair
5. call   say   thank   10. problem   long   boy

WRITE   *Write only words with the /o/ sound in the crossword puzzle.*

Down

1. the opposite of "employee"

3. the opposite of "short" (height)

5. Do you _____ to school?

6. This book _____ to me. It's mine!

10. The opposite of "short" (length)

Across

2. the opposite of "weak"

4. Wash the _____ (a pet).

7. the opposite of "big"

8. Please _____ me tomorrow.

9. "Be quiet!" Don't _____.

11. the opposite of "right"

12. I can't buy it; it _____ too much money.

16

Moving Day

- Review Chapter
- Final Test

LISTEN

Ann Porter is inviting Mona Boulos to go to the vacant apartment.

Ann: Hello, Mona. This is Ann Porter. I'm going to the apartment. I want to pay the manager for some supplies. Do you want to go with me? I want you to see the repairs.

Mona: Sure, what time do you want to go?

Ann: How about now?

Mona: Yes, OK. I'm just sitting here at home.

Ann: Good, I can pick you up in fifteen minutes.

Mona: Do you know how to get here?

Ann: Yes, I do. I have your address from your application form.

Mona: OK. See you in a few minutes.

UNDERSTAND   *Circle **True**, **False**, or **We don't know.***

1. Mona is calling Ann Porter.	True	False	We don't know.
2. Ann drives a car.	True	False	We don't know.
3. Ann wants Mona to see the apartment.	True	False	We don't know.
4. Mona knows how to get to the vacant apartment.	True	False	We don't know.
5. Mona has some free time.	True	False	We don't know.

WRITE   *Fill in the spaces with the words in the box.*

Mona Boulos and Sami Hamati meet at the apartment.

Mona: Hi, Sami, what __*are*__ you doing here?

Sami: I __'m__ working here. What about you?

Mona: You _____ standing in my new apartment!

Sami: Oh, really? The apartment _____ clean and ready for you.

Mona: Great! _____ you know where I _____ rent a truck?

Sami: Why _____ you need to rent a truck?

Mona: To move our furniture.

Sami: Try the Rent–a–Truck Company down the street.

Mona: _____ you have their address?

Sami: No, I _____. You _____ find it in the telephone book. _____ you need any help moving your furniture? I _____ ask some people at school to help.

Mona: Thanks, we _____ use some help.

Sami: Good. See you at school on Monday.

'm	's	are
do	don't	can

READ   Read the ads from the telephone book yellow pages.

Truck Renting and Leasing	Betty and Bob's Rent-a-Truck Service
Betty and Bob's Rent–a–Truck 4871 4th St. 988–4116	Call us first. We have very low rates.
	988–4116
Frank's Truck Rentals 19 Barney St. 976–1392	4871 Fourth Street
	Open 7 days a week
Fred's Car and Truck Rental Co. 996–7100 (see ads this page)	
Frank's Truck Rentals	Fred's Car and Truck Rental Company
We rent all kinds of equipment.	Local Rentals and One–way
Open Monday–Saturday	Open daily 9–6:30
8 a.m. to 5:30 p.m.	Rent by the hour, day, or week.
19 Barney Street	263 Main Street
976–1392	996–7100

PAIR PRACTICE   Talk with another student about the telephone ads above.

Student 1: What's the address/telephone number of ....?
Student 2: It's ....

PAIR PRACTICE   Talk with another student about the telephone ads above.

Student 1: Whose company rents ....?
Student 2: ....'s company does.

READ

Peter and Mona Boulos are renting a truck.

Clerk: May I help you?
Peter: We want to rent a truck.
Clerk: What size truck?
Peter: Not too small. We want to move some furniture.
Clerk: How long do you need it?
Peter: Half a day.
Clerk: Do you want to buy any extra insurance?
Peter: Yes, we do.
Clerk: Are you the only driver of the truck?
Peter: Yes, only me.
Clerk: OK. I want you to fill out this form. Give it to me when you finish.

WRITE   *Help Peter Boulos fill out the form.*

DRIVER'S LICENSE
P-92482

Peter Boulos   Date of Birth:
23 Shell Ave., #6   6/6/30
Los Angeles, CA
Expires: 1988
Signature:
Peter Boulos

RENTAL APPLICATION AND AGREEMENT

NAME: _____ STATE: _____

ADDRESS: _____ CITY: _____

TELEPHONE NUMBER: _____ DRIVER'S LICENSE NUMBER: _____

1. How long do you need the truck? _____

2. What size truck do you need? _____

3. Why do you need the truck? _____

4. Do you want any extra insurance? _____

5. How many drivers? _____

SIGNATURE: *Peter Boulos* _____ TODAY'S DATE: _____

PAIR PRACTICE   *Talk to another student about the floor plan below.*

Student 1: Where do you want .... to put the ....?
Student 2: I want .... to put .... in the ....

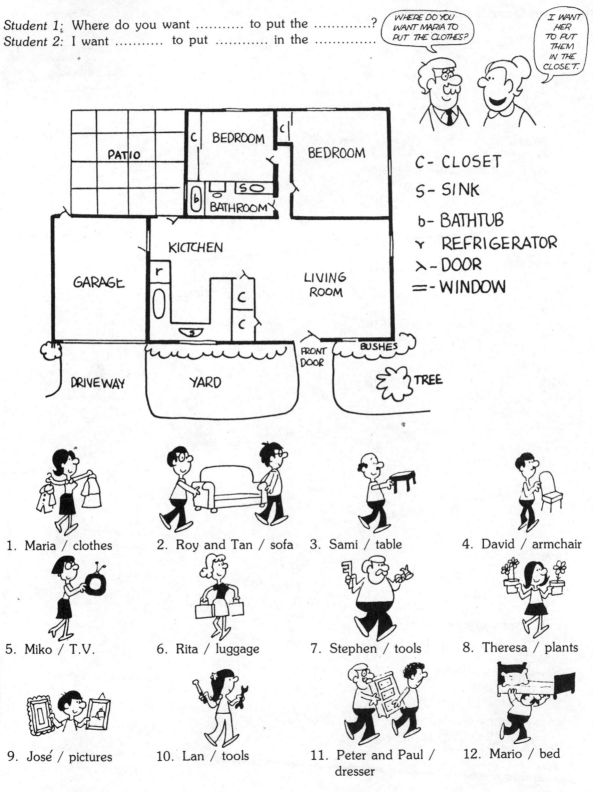

WHERE DO YOU WANT MARIA TO PUT THE CLOTHES?

I WANT HER TO PUT THEM IN THE CLOSET.

C – CLOSET
S – SINK
b – BATHTUB
Y – REFRIGERATOR
⋋ – DOOR
= – WINDOW

1. Maria / clothes
2. Roy and Tan / sofa
3. Sami / table
4. David / armchair
5. Miko / T.V.
6. Rita / luggage
7. Stephen / tools
8. Theresa / plants
9. José / pictures
10. Lan / tools
11. Peter and Paul / dresser
12. Mario / bed

DRAW   *Draw a picture of Mona's apartment building.*

Here's my apartment building.

1. Draw a car in the driveway.
2. Draw a bicycle next to the car.
3. Draw a large tree in the front of the apartment.
4. Draw some flowers around the tree.
5. Draw a small house to the right of Mona's apartment.
6. Draw a store to the left of the apartment.
7. Draw a big window on the front wall of the store.
8. Draw a "Help Wanted" sign in the store window.
9. Draw a fence between the store and Mona's apartment.
10. Draw some big white clouds over the buildings.
11. Draw ....

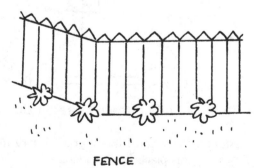

FENCE

READ

Mona and her friends are resting.

Mona: Is that the last piece of furniture?
Peter: Yes, it is.
Mona: Good! I have some sandwiches and drinks for you.
Maria: Just a moment, Mona. This is for you.
Mona: What is it?
Maria: It's a card and present from the students in our class. Please open it.

DICTATION   *Cover the sentence under the line. Write the dictation, and then check your writing.*

1. _____
   We want you to have this present.
2. _____
   It's for your new apartment.
3. _____
   We hope you like it.
4. _____
   From the students in your class.

Mona is putting the picture on the wall.

Mona: Peter and I thank you all very much. It's beautiful. What do you think about this place for the picture?
Peter: It's a great place and a great saying, too! "Home Sweet Home."

READ   *Make as many real words as you can from each of the puzzles. Begin with one of the consonants on the left, add one of the vowels or vowel combinations in the middle, and end with one of the consonants on the right. Use final **e** when necessary.*

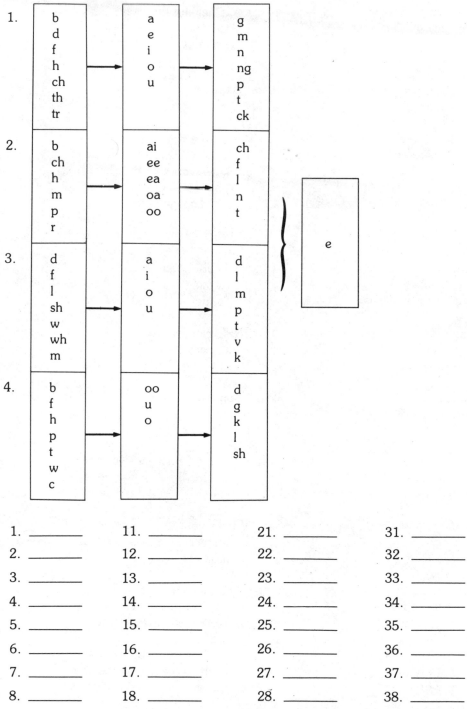

1. _____   11. _____   21. _____   31. _____   41. _____

2. _____   12. _____   22. _____   32. _____   42. _____

3. _____   13. _____   23. _____   33. _____   43. _____

4. _____   14. _____   24. _____   34. _____   44. _____

5. _____   15. _____   25. _____   35. _____   45. _____

6. _____   16. _____   26. _____   36. _____   46. _____

7. _____   17. _____   27. _____   37. _____   47. _____

8. _____   18. _____   28. _____   38. _____   48. _____

9. _____   19. _____   29. _____   39. _____   49. _____

10. _____   20. _____   30. _____   40. _____   50. _____

FINAL TEST   *Circle the correct answer.*

1. There _____ a bicycle in the garage.
   a. are   c. 's
   b. am   d. 're

2. How many people _____ here?
   a. are they   c. is there
   b. are there   d. there are

3. _____ a building in the photo?
   a. There is   c. There are
   b. Is there   d. Are there

4. Are there _____ old books for sale?
   a. any   c. an
   b. the   d. much

5. There are _____ for sale.
   a. a clean clothes   c. clothes clean
   b. clean clothes   d. cleans clothes

6. How much _____ cost?
   a. do it   c. is it
   b. does it   d. are they

7. When it's 9:45, it's _____.
   a. quarter to 9   c. half past 9
   b. nine sharp   d. a quarter to 10

8. The girl takes the bus _____.
   a. to school   c. at school
   b. in school   d. school

9. Let's stand _____ the window.
   a. to   c. on
   b. at   d. too

10. Mario Corral works _____.
    a. downtown   c. in downtown
    b. at downtown   d. to downtown

11. Maria comes _____ a little tired.
    a. at home   c. to home
    b. in home   d. home

12. Excuse me, _____ this ladder?
    a. are you using   c. do you using
    b. is you using   d. you using

13. Are you working now? _____.
    a. Yes, we are   c. Yes, you are
    b. Yes, they are   d. Yes, she is

14. Joe is helping the boss _____.
    a. last Monday   c. last week
    b. yesterday   d. now

15. _____ you need any help?
    a. Does   c. Are
    b. Do   d. Is

16. What's she doing? _____.
    a. She's working   c. She working
    b. She's work   d. She works

17. _____ luggage is this?
    a. Who   c. Whose
    b. Who's   d. How's

18. Is this your bag? Yes, _____.
    a. it's mine   c. it's my
    b. it's me   d. it's your

19. These clothes are _____.
    a. to big   c. too big
    b. too much big d. two big

20. I don't know some _____ these people.
    a. for   c. of
    b. from   d. off

21. Do _____ relatives live here?
    a. you   c. you're
    b. your   d. they're

22. What's your _____ name?
    a. brother   c. brother's
    b. brothers   d. brothers'

23. My aunt's husband is my _____.
    a. cousin   c. grandfather
    b. brother-in-law   d. uncle

24. Excuse me, are you the owner _____?
    a. of the store's   c. the store
    b. the store's   d. of the store

25. What _____ is the car?
    a. of the color   c. color
    b. color's   d. colors'

26. What's the _____ name?
    a. owner's   c. owner
    b. owners'   d. owners

27. _____ an apartment for rent?
    a. Has you   c. Do you have
    b. You do have   d. Do you has

28. The apartment _____ two bedrooms.
    a. have   c. have't
    b. has   d. don't have

29. Does the apartment have draperies?
    _____.
    a. Yes, it have   c. Yes, it does
    b. Yes, it is   d. Yes, it do

30. _____ pets do you have?
    a. How much   c. How
    b. How many   d. How money

31. I want _____ to you.
    a. too talk   c. to talk
    b. talks   d. talk

32. Call a painter. I want _____ to paint every room.
    a. them   c. his
    b. him   d. he

33. Ann doesn't want to spend _____ money.
    a. many   c. too many
    b. a lot d. a lot of

34. What's _____ with the bathroom?
    a. the matter   c. matter
    b. matters   d. a matter

35. I have money _____ some materials.
    a. buying   c. to buy
    b. to buying   d. for buy

36. They need some _____ to fix the bathroom.
    a. equipments   c. tool
    b. equipment   d. supply

37. Do you _____ to fix this?
    a. knowing   c. know how
    b. now how   d. know what

38. Why do you _____ to rent a truck?
    a. to want   c. wants
    b. want   d. wanting

39. Hello, what can I _____ for you?
    a. to does   c. to do
    b. does   d. do

40. Thank you _____ the beautiful present.
    a. for   c. of
    b. from   d. off

41. _____ you come to school yesterday?
    a. Will   c. Did
    b. Is   d. Do

42. Sami and David _____ hard yesterday.
    a. work   c. works
    b. worked   d. is working

43. Did Paul _____ to the store?
    a. go   c. going
    b. went   d. goes

44. Paul _____ to buy some paint.
    a. go   c. going
    b. went   d. is went

45. Where _____ he buy the paint?
    a. do   c. did
    b. is   d. are

46. He _____ the paint on sale.
    a. buying   c. buy
    b. buyed   d. bought

47. He _____ to school yesterday.
    a. does't come   c. didn't come
    b. isn't coming d. don't come

48. He _____ to this country in 1983.
    a. came   c. will come
    b. come   d. comes

49. _____ you tired?
    a. Is   c. Did
    b. Are   d. Do

50. This _____ the last item of this test.
    a. not   c. does
    b. is   d. doesn't

CHALLENGE   *After you correct the test, calculate your grade below.*

- *Write the number of **correct** answers in the box below.*

> CORRECT ANSWERS

- *Multiply the number of correct answers by 2.*

> CORRECT ANSWERS   x   2   =

- *Find your letter grade below.*

90	to	100	= A	(excellent)
75	to	89	= B	(above average)
60	to	74	= C	(average)
45	to	59	= D	(below average)
0	to	44	= F	(failure)

- *Write your final grade in the box below.*

> MY FINAL GRADE:

WORD LIST

about 27
accountant 32, 88
across 87
activities 138
ad 84
address 87
adult 24, 116
after 47
again 91, 204
age 59
agency 156
airport 158, 204
album 216
all 116
all right 26
always 120
am 27
ambulance 56
an 24, 32
and 24
answer 146
antique 132, 226
any 154
apartment 49, 76
apples 25
appliances 166
application 87, 145
apply for 146, 234
appointment 166
appreciate 135
April 60, 105
are 24
aren't 45
around 72, 93
arrange 101
arrive 238
at 24
August 60, 105
aunt 216
auto 32
avenue 76
average 223
back 66, 91
bags 204
balance 131
bank 62, 64, 156
barber 156
baseball 107
bathroom 166
be 72

beach 126, 158
beginning 66
behind 91, 126
beige 204
bell 27, 70
belong to 204
belt 207
between 91, 126
bicycle 152
big 49
bill 107, 130
birth 59, 76
birthday 60
black 91
blouse 207
blue 91
blueprint 36
book 7
bookkeeper 208
boots 91
born 58
both 157, 216
bother 88
bought 238
boulevard 76
break 24
broken 152, 230
broom 15
brother 49
brother-in-law 216
brown 91
bulb 101
bulletin board 36
bus stop 158
business 64
busy 101
bye 27
calculate 132
calendar 60, 105
call 132
calls 116
came 238
can 64, 116
can't 64
card 29, 76
care 138
careful 49, 72
carefully 66
carpets 166
cashier 32, 88, 146

catering 24
ceiling 16
center 138
cents 24
chair 7
chalk 36
chalkboard 7, 36
change 24, 120
cheap 223
check 130, 146
choose 101
chores 107
church 157
city 76
claim 207
class 24
classroom 44
clean 49, 101
clean out 152
clean up 72
clock 7
clogged 230
close 66
clothes 64, 208
coat 207
coffee 24
coffee shop 64
coin 131
color 132
colored 208
combination 55
come 29, 67
come on 44
company 116, 156
complicated 216
computer 64
condition 223
condominium 169
convenient 166
cookies 25
corner 36, 152
correct 66
cosmetics 207
cost 130
counseling 76, 96
counselor 94
country 34
cousins 216
cracked 230
crew 230

cube 101
customer 154
dad 116
damaged 230
dangerous 49
date 60, 76
December 60, 105
deliver 238
den 166
dentist 156
department 88, 144
desk 7, 36
dictionary 36
died 61
difference 157
dime 131
dinner 116
directory 65
distance 116
does 117
doesn't 117
dollar 130
don't 70
door 7
doughnuts 130
down 29, 92
downstairs 92
draftsman 49
drain 230
draperies 166
drive 76
driveway 154
drop 72
drugstore 85
dryer 132
dust 101
each 130
early 120
east 76
eight 37
electric 156
electrician 32
electronic 88
eleven 37
emergency 56
employee 116
employment 145
enough 152, 238
equals 37
equipment 88, 146

ESL 24
every 120
everybody 66
excellent 223
excuse 24, 56
exercise 70, 138
experience 234
extra 230
facilities 138
factory 147
false 24
family 125, 216
fan 230
far 64
favor 70
February 60, 105
fifth 59, 64
fill out 76
find 138
fine 44
finish 70, 126
fire department 56
first 59, 64, 76
fit 91, 208
five 37
fix 101, 146, 230
fixtures 234
flight 204
floor 16
flower pot 152
food 69, 132
for 47
forget 73, 107
found 64, 204
four 37
fourth 59, 64
free 166
friendly 49
from 29
frost-free 223
fun 107
furniture 64, 132
game 107
garage 152
garage sale 151
garbage 107
garbage can 152
get 66
get ready 101
get up 120